ROUTLEDGE LIBRARY EDITIONS:
URBAN STUDIES

Volume 18

GROUP WORK WITH SUBURBIA'S CHILDREN

GROUP WORK WITH SUBURBIA'S CHILDREN

Difference, Acceptance and Belonging

Edited by
ANDREW MALEKOFF

Routledge
Taylor & Francis Group

LONDON AND NEW YORK

First published in 1991 by The Haworth Press, Inc.

This edition first published in 2018
by Routledge
2 Park Square, Milton Park, Abingdon, Oxon OX14 4RN

and by Routledge
711 Third Avenue, New York, NY 10017

Routledge is an imprint of the Taylor & Francis Group, an informa business

British Library Cataloguing in Publication Data
A catalogue record for this book is available from the British Library

ISBN: 978-1-138-89482-2 (Set)
ISBN: 978-1-315-09987-3 (Set) (ebk)
ISBN: 978-1-138-05130-0 (Volume 18) (hbk)
ISBN: 978-1-138-05134-8 (Volume 18) (pbk)
ISBN: 978-1-315-16834-0 (Volume 18) (ebk)

Publisher's Note
The publisher has gone to great lengths to ensure the quality of this reprint but points out that some imperfections in the original copies may be apparent.

Disclaimer
The publisher has made every effort to trace copyright holders and would welcome correspondence from those they have been unable to trace.

Group Work
with Suburbia's
Children:
Difference, Acceptance
and Belonging

Andrew Malekoff
Editor

The Haworth Press
New York • London

Group Work with Suburbia's Children: Difference, Acceptance and Belonging has also been published as *Social Work with Groups*, Volume 14, Number 1 1991.

The Haworth Press, Inc. 10 Alice Street, Binghamton, NY 13904-1580
EUROSPAN/Haworth, 3 Henrietta Street, London WC2E 8LU England

Library of Congress Cataloging-in-Publication Data

Group work with suburbia's children : difference, acceptance, and belonging/ Andrew Malekoff, editor.
    p. cm.
    "Has also been published as Social work with groups, volume 14, number 1, 1991"—CIP t.p. verso
    Includes bibliographical references.
    ISBN 1-56024-100-4
    1. Social group work—United States. 2. Suburban life—United States. 3. Family social work—United States. I. Malekoff, Andrew.
HV45.G7317
362.7—dc20

                        90-49255
                          CIP

Group Work
with Suburbia's Children:
Difference, Acceptance
and Belonging

CONTENTS

BOOK REVIEWS

ABOUT THE EDITOR

Andrew Malekoff, MSW, directs the Suburban Family Life Center and Substance Abuse Treatment and Prevention Services for the North Shore Child and Family Guidance Center in Roslyn Heights, New York. His first experience as a group worker was while serving as a VISTA volunteer in Grand Island, Nebraska. He has published several articles related to group work with children and adolescents, the development of neighborhood networks, and the creation of an action oriented research approach to promote community change. Mr. Malekoff was appointed by the Board of Directors of the American Orthopsychiatric Association to chair the Study Group on Adolescence sponsored by the AOA. He has recently been named Associate Editor of *Social Work with Groups* and to serve on the Board of Directors of the Advancement of Social Work with Groups (AASWG).

This book is dedicated to my family.

Group Work
with Suburbia's Children:
Difference, Acceptance
and Belonging

Foreword

It is gratifying to find in this special collection of papers the extent to which group work has become a method of choice in mental health agencies serving families and children in suburbia. These agencies are recognizing that alienation and isolation are prominent societal factors in the inability of families to cope with contemporary pressures and that service in the small group has powerful therapeutic possibilities, in work both with the children and with their parents. This has been a concern and commitment of the Co-editors and Advisory Board of *Social Work with Groups* and its contributors and readers during the fourteen years since its inception in 1978 and throughout the decades of the development of social group work as one of the central methodologies of professional social work. We welcome this addition to the *Social Work with Groups Series*.

The compendium of human problems, including violence, abuse, suicide, depression, that are presented to the suburban agency is indeed shocking. The problems are surprisingly similar to those to be found in the impoverished communities and ghettos of the inner cities. Clearly economic advantages are insufficient to meet the anomie that pervades the society as a whole. The hope on the horizon is that we are reaching out, in the words of Marion Levine, "to provide at the edges what we have lost at the center."

As Co-editors of the publication we have agreed with our Special Editor, Andrew Malekoff, to include the programmatic listing of a suburban agency's full array of group activities offered to serve youth and their families. The listing in itself is worthy of the consideration of our readers. We feel certain that professionals in other parts of the country will want to explore some of these ideas or exchange similar ideas with the authors of this volume.

In a profession that has gone overboard with specialization in regard to pathology, we find in this volume an appreciation for the

xiii

generic value of the small group in communal and individual growth and development. While the specific articles speak to the skill and knowledge of the professional workers, more important is the fact that the agencies are recognizing that the empowerment of suburban youth and their families lies with the common human need for social closeness. Without feeling some part of a close group of humans that matter, and to whom one matters, people in suburbia as elsewhere can not survive. The view of the therapeutic potential of the small group has never been tied to or excluded from any particular psychological condition or philosophy. Its significance in serving social psychological needs is clearly illustrated in this volume.

Andrew Malekoff's literary gift in reporting his own professional group work is reflected in this volume. In the final article he brings to life and helps us to understand the tenderness with which he works with children, responding to their needs, joys, pains, and possibilities. His design for the volume and selection of articles reinforces our confidence in inviting him to prepare this special collection on group work with suburbia's children.

This is an arresting volume and one that we commend to the readers of *Social Work with Groups* and to the social work profession. It is to be contemplated, not only as illustration of what social group workers can do directly, but also as what we have to offer to our colleagues — casework, community and policy practitioners. The commitment of every social worker to the creating of small group affiliation within all communities is necessary in order to validate and enrich the societal mission of our profession.

Catherine P. Papell
Beulah Rothman

This Volume was prepared and the Foreword written before Beulah Rothman's death in August 1990.

Preface

A home in the suburbs: for most Americans reared in the depression an impossible dream; then, suddenly, after World War II a reality. Government loans on generous terms to veterans, and government guaranteed loans to others, spur the exodus from the city. Areas once completely rural burgeon with new housing. Virtually every young couple wants to move. To be a homeowner, even with a thirty year mortgage, is to feel somehow freer, to be more truly American.

Twenty years later, social critics and folk singers will sneer at the "ticky tacky" houses and the people to be found there. For those who had moved to the suburbs originally, however, the feelings that brought them out of the city remained. Tract home or colonial, be its yard great or small, a suburban home was still seen as a guarantor of respectability, comfort and tranquility.

To be sure, members of ethnic, racial and religious minorities made their way into the suburbs, past the maze of restrictive housing covenants, only with difficulty. Black and Hispanic suburbanites were clearly a rarity and made to feel unwanted. But even white city dwellers of "acceptable" religious or ethnic background who made it into the "developments" and "garden cities" often discovered that the move rarely eliminated already existing family problems and sometimes brought with it new tensions, as well. One social worker who occupied himself during the 1950s with the struggles of newly-prosperous, skilled blue collar workers who had moved into one of his city's affluent suburbs, was reminded of the stunned condition of the uprooted populations of post-war Europe. "My clients are surprisingly like Displaced Persons in many ways," he observed. "They may be living only ten miles from their former homes, but they've been separated from surroundings which were familiar to them for a couple of generations at least, where

xv

they knew what was expected of them. Now they're culturally and emotionally disoriented, many of them, profoundly so.''

The best of village life, which the suburb was to afford the home-owners of the 'fifties, and which they had observed in pre-World War II movies—all white picket fences and pleasant, well-heeled neighbors, as in the Andy Hardy series, starring Mickey Rooney and Judy Garland—remained elusive for many. Indeed, some group workers who had previously worked in settlement houses, but were now employed in outreach work with groups of children and youth in the suburbs were struck by a certain irony in the situation. After all, the original settlement houses were designed to bring the neigh-borliness of village life to the socially disorganized slums of the city. In this way the anomie experienced by industrial slum dwell-ers, themselves torn away from their village roots in America or Europe, was to be counteracted. Emotional wholeness and intellec-tual progress for individuals and greater opportunity for these ex-ploited industrial workers to take collective action on their own be-half were to be the results. Now, however, in the suburb, the up-to-date version of the prosperous American village, some of the residents were finding this new village life one of alienation and confusion. Examination of the experiences of workers in clinical agencies, sponsoring suburban group work in the decades immedi-ately following World War II makes this apparent. The emotional neglect of children, the social closeting of the physically handi-capped, school failures and school phobia, the rejection of the emo-tionally disturbed, and delinquency, even of the group variety,— these are some of the problems that will be especially remembered by the few trained group workers who found their way to these settings. These workers will also remember trying to deal with their own projections, as they struggled to control their punitive feelings toward client-members who were often so emotionally demanding and needy when, in material terms, they "had so much."

Today's suburban group worker functions in a social environ-ment where the contrast between the original aspirations of the resi-dents and the severity of the behavioral problems manifested by some of them is even more striking than previously. Few group workers of an earlier era would have expected to encounter such all too common contemporary phenomena as drug dealing in suburban grade schools, or extensive sexual experimentation at an age when those of an older generation had not even considered dating. Group workers, themselves, can live in the suburbs and be aware of the satisfactions suburban living may bring. The fact that existence for today's suburban residents is something less than idyllic, however, is something that they are made aware of, not only through their professional work, but whenever they sit down to read the evening paper. A report in one suburban newspaper, the day these lines were written, begins: "Three youths walked into a math class at the high school yesterday and tried to assault a student while a stunned teacher and a dozen classmates watched." Later, the article concludes with the school superintendent's reassurances to the reporter, including the fact that all doors except the main entrance are secured after students arrive for class, and nothing serious could happen because, even if someone gets in, "There are lots of teachers around." Meanwhile, on the same day, a large urban daily headlines, in banner type, "Poverty soars in the suburbs," and describes how newly poor suburbanites not only suffer, materially, but are so deeply ashamed that they pretend they do not need help.

This is the arena in which suburban social group work is being shaped. As seen in the following pages it involves enormously hard work as well as considerable professional imagination and ingenuity. Its description should inspire, not a search for neat solutions or packaged programs, but doggedness in our continuing efforts at experimentation and improvisation as we work to reduce human suffering through the group experience.

Ralph L. Kolodny
Professor Emeritus
Boston University School of Social Work

Introduction

The earliest vision of this special volume, *Group Work with Suburbia's Children*, was of a collection of writings on *difference, acceptance and belonging*. Not as romantic as images of the "suburban dream," this theme represents the reality and the promise of community life.

The collection of articles herein attempts to describe life in the suburbs from diverse vantage points, to evoke a feeling of what life is like for some of the children and their families living in these communities and to demonstrate the practice and value of group work within this context.

Nassau County, Long Island, a suburb of New York City serves as the backdrop for the first three articles by Levine, Wilson and López. These authors take us beyond the "dream," highlighting the unique role of group work along the way. Levine sets the tone for the special collection with a discussion of a group work response to alienation and the changing family. Wilson describes aspects of the black experience in suburbia, providing specific recommendations and cautionary notes for group work intervention. And, López illustrates the plight of immigrant youth in their struggle to adapt to a new homeland.

The suburbs of Central Ohio and Ontario, Canada, provide the settings for the next two articles which detail time limited group approaches with special populations of troubled youth. In the former Harper and Shillito describe a carefully detailed educational/ support group model for female adolescents with eating disorders. This is followed by Walsh, Richardson and Cardey who thoughtfully and creatively demonstrate "the curative power of fantasy in working with children".

The guest editor has a hand in the final three articles. In the first he explores avenues for engaging parents whose children are in group treatment. This is followed by a collaboration with Kolodny in which the authors develop a portrait of the lonely child which crosses back and forth between suburban and urban landscapes (Long Island, New York and Boston, Massachusetts). The final article, conceived as the special collection's epilogue, is a reverie on difference, acceptance and belonging as viewed through the eyes of the author and a young man recalling his earlier days as a member in a boys' group.

This special collection represents an attempt to temper some of the more romantic images of life in the suburbs, especially as reflected through children's experiences. In addition, the purpose is to present various prospects and possibilities for group work intervention and to demonstrate, through anecdotal material, the promise which they represent.

Andrew Malekoff
North Shore Child
and Family Guidance Center
Roslyn Heights, NY 11577

Group Work:
Antidote to Alienation
During a Time of Family Transition

Marion Levine

SUMMARY. The purpose of this article is to describe the process through which a voluntary agency develops its philosophy and defines its own values and beliefs. The development of a comprehensive structure of group work services is presented. The circular and reciprocal nature of the helping relationship is emphasized.

The family is a hot issue. Judging by the proliferation of magazine cover stories, television features, talk show discussions, academic research, and public policy discourse being devoted to the state of the American family, it seems safe to say that what civil rights and Vietnam were to the Sixties, and women's rights and the environment were to the Seventies, family issues became to the Eighties. People care about their own families, of course, but of late they also seem terribly concerned about the *idea* of family and the future of family life in this country.

So begins Letty Cottin Pogrebin in her book *Family Politics: Love and Politics on an Intimate Frontier.*[1]

Brigette and Peter L. Berger in their opening page *The War Over the Family: Capturing The Middle Ground* lead off with:

Marion Levine, ACSW, is Executive Director of the North Shore Child and Family Guidance Center, Roslyn Heights, NY.

3

The family has become a problem. This observation is widely made today, in America as well as in other societies, to the point where it has become commonplace. Needless to say, people who make the observation differ among themselves about the nature of the problem and about possible solutions; indeed what is a solution to some appears as yet another facet of the problem to others.[2]

PROVIDING AT THE "EDGE"
WHAT HAS BEEN LOST IN THE "CENTER"

As a suburban mental health center serving children, youth and their families, North Shore Child and Family Guidance Center, has lived through almost 35 years of changes in family life in the communities we serve. One of the ways in which the staff keeps in tune with current family patterns is through an understanding that our organization is a microcosm of our suburban life. Once a problem, repeatedly presented, can be cited as a statistic, we examine what is happening with families in our communities, and ask ourselves: What is contributing to the development and the continuance of these symptoms?

A recent listing of 100 consecutive cases admitted to the Clinic revealed:

- In almost two-thirds of the families there was a seriously depressed member; fourteen of these are children under the age of 12; 19 are adolescents;
- Twenty-seven reported sexual or physical abuse;
- Twenty-two presented with suicidal ideation; 7 of these were under 11 years of age;
- Seventeen individuals presented with problems that were at least partially reactive to a suicide attempt, or actual suicide, by a member of the family;
- In 12 cases, either the patient or a family member had been previously hospitalized for severe psychiatric disturbance, some of them more than once;
- Over 40 parents abuse alcohol or drugs;
- Seven parents are or have been in prison;

• Violence is evident in 19 cases; in 15 it is a parent who is violent.

The theme that pervades many of our applications is the dysfunctional adaptation of parents and children to painful changes in their life circumstances. Many youngsters we see have constitutional problems that would present difficulties no matter what strengths the families have. But many more, presently, are reacting to extraordinary fear and losses early in life. These fears and losses rob them of the sense of safety and security necessary to meet the struggles that are a natural part of growth. These youngsters feel betrayed by those they trusted to protect them, and they respond with punitive rage or in self-destructive acts in an effort to disengage from their pain.

Our daily concern, at work, is what is happening to families. We deal with the symptoms clinically; we attempt to address the "context" through action-oriented research surveys* designed to raise community consciousness on matters of concern to children and families. More and more it feels like the "breakdown" in the family as protector and mediator for children is not just evident at the "edges" of our communities, but rather that the "breakdown" is threatening the center itself. No longer, as per 20 years ago, are we referring to multi-problem families as only those who are near poverty and historically disadvantaged in our society.

We have a new poor in the single parent population. "Doing your own thing" is too often a substitute for caring about others. We have those who "haven't got time for the pain," who turn on and tune out. We see many whose internal controls are dissolved through alcohol and substance abuse, who have easy access to weapons, and who do not, in their altered states of consciousness, abhor, but rather embrace violence as a means to solving problems. Clearly, serious disturbance, severe depression and dislocation, violence have become commonplace with "helping" professionals experiencing increasingly incredible pressures as they attempt to respond to the demands.

---

*For a description of the action research approach as applied in this organization refer to "Hope or Despair: Suburbia's Children Look into the Future" (by Andrew Malekoff) *Social Work with Groups* Volume 13, Number 3 1990.

It would please me to find a politically potent alliance of pro-family groups who are successfully withstanding the devastating effects of hi-tech, instant and continuous change, drug saturation, loss of leadership and role models, marketing experts mind manipulation techniques, and most importantly loss of faith that there will be a future. Unfortunately, we are seeing more persons than ever who are feeling isolated, and the victims of overwhelming circumstances.

Presently, our job has become one of helping to empower people — of helping them to move toward mastery despite threats to their safety and security, and limited resources. More and more our roles have shifted from probing and reflecting to providing structure, stability, consistency and predictability, to insuring opportunities for attachments through a proliferation of support groups and mutual aid networks. Essentially, we are providing at the edges what has been lost in the center.

ANOMIE, VALUES AND SOCIAL CONTEXT

What I would like to do to further this discussion is (1) examine what we're seeing in a broader theoretical context and (2) attempt to describe our practice within the parameters of its theoretical underpinnings — and more. "And more" refers to building on theory to extend its application in a way that expresses our organization's philosophy, and reflects our identity.

Emile Durkheim, a clinical social theorist argued that, at its core every human society is a moral community, and that in the absence of shared moral values, a society must begin to disintegrate. To quote:

> It is not true, then, that human activity can be released from all restraint. Nothing in the world can enjoy such a privilege. All existence being a part of the universe is relative to the remainder; its nature and method of manifestation accordingly depend not only on itself but on other beings, who consequently restrain and regulate it. Here there are only differences of degree and form between the mineral realm and the thinking person. Man's characteristic privilege is that the bond he accepts is not physical but moral; that is, social. He is governed not by

a material environment brutally imposed on him, but by a conscience superior to his own, the superiority of which he feels.
Because the greater, better part of his existence transcends the
body, he escapes the body's yoke, but is subject to that of
society. But when society is disturbed by some painful crisis
or by beneficent but abrupt transitions, it is momentarily in-
capable of exercising this influence; thence come the sudden
rises in the curve of suicides. . . .[3]

Durkheim's work *Suicide* demonstrates that human behavior although it may seem very individual, can be understood only by
investigating the *social context* in which the behavior takes place.
Anomie is viewed as a condition of social normlessness in which
norms are weak, conflicting or absent. Anomie causes societies to
become disorganized and individuals to lose a sense of shared values and norms. Durkheim's central thesis was that the more a person is integrated into intimate social groups, the less likely he or she
is to commit suicide.[4]

Our thesis is that the "values vacuum" inherent in the anything
goes, do your own thing, narcissistic search for personal fulfillment
era represents a contemporary version of anomie. There may be
much that is shared—but that is primarily trends in the pursuit of
instant gratification; form not substance has become idealized. Attachments are tenuous or too often non-existent. Individuals are less
meaningfully involved in group life and often only marginally, (if at
all) committed to being a part of a cohesive social unit.

The crisis in family life stimulated by a combination of abrupt
transitions (i.e., impact of women's movement among others)
weakened society's capacity to provide the "superior conscience"
for the individual. Previously, it had been the traditional family
whose role it was to be the bearer and transmitter of shared moral
values to the next generation.

Maxine Schnall, in her book *Limits* decries the loneliness and
isolation that have evolved via cultural trends of recent decades:

In pursuing liberation without understanding the *need for limits* we wind up with *less* freedom than we had before. By un-
doing all the old patterns of intimacy in friendships, love affairs, and marriage and also discarding as too restrictive of our

'human potential' many of those traditional values espoused by our parents — duty, honor, responsibility — what have we gained?

We've gained the right to live our lives solely on the basis of personal choice but have cut out from under us any supports to give those choices meaning and direction. We have set ourselves free to do virtually anything we choose, but we have no way of judging the validity, morality, or even sanity of our choices in a culture where everything is right and nothing is wrong. . . .

. . . .the guilt conflicts that were the root of our social neurosis in the repressive victorian era have been replaced, by virtue of overchoice, with depression and alienation. . . .[5]

Durkheim pointed out that unlimited desires are insatiable by definition.

All man's pleasure in acting, moving, and exerting himself implies the sense that his efforts are not in vain and that by walking he had advanced. However, one does not advance when one walks toward no goal, or — which is the same thing — when his goal is infinity.[6]

In a similar vein Marian Wright Edelman, founder of the Children's Defense Fund, cites educator Dr. Benjamin E. Mays in her book, *Families in Peril: An Agenda for Social Change*:

It must be borne in mind that the tragedy of life doesn't lie in not reaching your goal. The tragedy lies in having no goal to reach.[7]

When attainable goals, values, purpose, attachments to cohesive social units are lacking, the "hole" within the individual is bottomless. Then we see the constant searching for the next piece of excitement, for within this context, the more one has the more one wants, since satisfaction received only stimulates instead of filling needs.

FROM SYMPTOM TO STATISTIC:
THE CREATION OF A MEDIATING STRUCTURE

If we reframe the list of problems presented by 100 families that were cited earlier in this paper, in 88 of these depression and/or alienation could be seen as a core issue. Those who are in touch with this often attempt suicide. In the majority of the other cases, we deal with what the psychiatric jargon refers to as "impulse — disordered" individuals. These individuals move from impulse to action with no pause for reflection. They have no sense of boundaries, and no connection to the impact of their behavior on others; they are self-destructive at the same time as they are hurtful to others. To interrupt their pattern we must move them to reflection before action. Many resist these efforts — for good reason — for when they stop running or drinking or lashing out, they get in touch with the pain of depression and their sense of alienation.

In an ever-shifting, fast changing society, highly dependent on consumerism, the goal of the corporate world often is to keep stimulating individuals to want more — and to promise that this one more thing is definitely essential to fill your needs. The competition of the "quick fix, pain alleviation" advertisements is formidable when what you offer requires delayed gratification, struggle and pain.

It is within the midst of this combination of forces that a voluntary agency dedicated to serving children, youth and families must develop its philosophy and define its own values and beliefs. Retrospectively, our choices were motivated — conscious or not — by the formulations described above. Essentially we *expanded* on family systems theory to connect people to one another, and in the shared problem-solving tasks, have them develop a set of standards and beliefs that they could live with and by.

"Systems theory," as succinctly summarized by Danuta Mostwin in the *Social Dimension of Family Treatment*

> is basically concerned with the study of the living organisms and/or social organizations that depend for their existence on external situations and on the interrelationship between themselves and the environment . . . [8]

In order for us as clinicians to enlarge the family systems idea, we placed the child within the context of family *and* other social groups or institutions (i.e., schools, day care centers, neighborhood, protective services, etc.). Then, in doing an assessment we could make an intervention in one or more points in an effort to connect "actors" in the child's life into a nurturing network or create a collaborative team.

Once we looked at a situation in this way, the possibilities for our interaction with the community enlarged. In a sense we might view ourselves as a mediating structure defined by Berger and Neuhaus as

> those institutions standing between the individual in his private life and the large institutions of public life . . .[9]

Because we were interacting with other community groups and institutions in relation to cases, we were often made aware of problems and issues in those systems. Our willingness to collaborate on behalf of *a* child then moved to our providing services to day care workers or other professionals on behalf of *the* children in their center or community. Such collaboration, as William Schwartz points out in his work on the mediating function between client and system,

> may involve conflict, cooperation, confrontation, negotiation or any other form of exchange emerging from the realities of the situation . . . the demand is not for conciliation but for a realistic exchange . . .[10]

The conceptual framework described above began as a response to cases. However, the viewing of symptoms as manifestations of adaptive patterns (within a systems model) led us to collect statistics on symptoms as indicators of what was happening in our communities.

GROUP WORK: THE ANTIDOTE

Once we made our beliefs clear — that connectedness, collaboration, developing caring networks was important in these times, then groups would cooperate when we would do an action-oriented research survey. It was from the collaboration with other groups, and from the effects of the surveys that all of our suburban family life preventive programs were created. (See Appendix I for listing.) All of these programs are organized around a family group or support network model — in an effort to deal with the prevailing sense of isolation and alienation evident in our communities.

Secondly, they are organized around an "empowerment" rather than "pathology" orientation. This enlarges on the "collaborators" notion (professionals and clients become partners in problem-solving) as well as addresses the issue of powerlessness that is evident in many depressed individuals. The circular and reciprocal nature of the helping relationship, deeply imbedded in the group work tradition, provides a foundation for the collaboration described above.[11]

In the clinic, while we continue a family orientation, in recent years there has been a shift within that framework to increasing group treatment. Initially, our view was that this was the "treatment of choice" for impulse-disorder individuals. However, within the context of this discussion it is clear that this shift has much broader significance. James A. Garland and Ralph L. Kolodny in their book *The Treatment of Children Through Social Group Work: A Developmental Approach*, assert that

> group treatment is not just a clinical response to specific pathological entities presented by clients, but a general social movement and an attempt to restore intimate, lasting, face to face experiences for members of society in general.[12]

Our recognition of the social conditions that are contributing to the breakdown of the individual, of families, or neighborhoods has stimulated a response to fill a need that is lacking elsewhere. Groups (see Appendix II for clinic group listings) are providing: (1) boundaries; (2) structure; (3) an opportunity for attachments; (4) a set of standards; (5) a developing system of beliefs that are shared; (6) a role as a member of a cohesive social unit and; (7) an opportunity for thoughtful consideration of replacing one's unrealistic expectations with attainable and meaningful goals.

CONCLUSION:
VISION, COMMITMENT AND COUNTERFORCE

When one reviews the facts of our present social condition — at least as experienced in a contemporary human services agency — it is more than depressing. What keeps us from total despair is a vision, and a shared set of values and beliefs. We, as a staff, recreate for ourselves a cohesive social unit of which we are a part (see Appendix III). Our development of a caring working environment enables us, in turn, to share the benefits of our support network with individuals, families, and community groups with whom we interact. In a time of transition it is important to remind ourselves that, usually, once a force propels a society too far in a direction, a counterforce often gets set in motion to address the impact of that force. Within the context of Hegelian philosophical thought, thesis/antithesis/synthesis is an ever evolving historical process. The "values vacuum" is beginning to be addressed in some segments of our communities. This could be the seeds of the beginning of a recognition that life loses meaning in a society when there is an "absence of shared moral values" and a lack of commitment to a cohesive social group.

NOTES

1. Letty Cottin Pogrebin, *Family Politics* (New York: McGraw-Hill Book Company, 1983), p. 2.

2. Brigette Berger and Peter L. Berger, *The War Over The Family* (New York: Anchor Press/Doubleday, 1983), p. 3.

3. Emile Durkheim, *Suicide* (New York: The Free Press, 1966), p. 252.

4. *Ibid*.

5. Maxine Schnall, *Limits* (New York: Clarkson N. Potter, Inc./Publishers, 1981), p. 708.

6. *op. cit.* Suicide, p. 248.

7. Marian Wright Edelman, *Families in Peril: An Agenda for Social Change*

(Cambridge, Massachusetts, and London, England: Harvard University Press, 1987), p. 113.

8. Danuta Mostwin, *Social Dimension of Family Treatment* (Washington, D.C.: National Association of Social Workers, Inc., 1980), p. 27

9. Peter L. Berger and Richard John Neuhaus, *To Empower People* (Washington, D.C.: American Enterprise Institute for Public Policy Research, 1977), p. 2.

10. William Schwartz, *"Between Client and System: Mediating Function," Theories of Social Work with Groups* (New York: Columbia University Press, 1976), p. 185.

11. William Schwartz, "The Group Work Tradition and Social Work Practice," *The Legacy of William Schwartz: Group Practice as Shared Interaction* (eds. Alex Gitterman and Lawrence Shulman), (New York: Haworth Press, 1985/86), p. 20.

12. James A. Garland and Ralph L. Kolodny, *The Treatment of Children Through Social Group Work: A Developmental Approach* (Uncorrected Advance proof). (Boston, Massachusetts: Charles River Books, 1981), pp. 111-112.

APPENDIX I:
FAMILY LIFE SERVICES

Early Childhood Training Institute

The number of infants and toddlers requiring day care has increased dramatically in recent years. Forces such as abuse, poor parenting, single parent needs, all serve to increase the demands on Day Care and Nursery School providers. It is the goal of the Early Childhood Training Institute to meet this need with a high level of training, education, and professional support for caregivers of infants and toddlers.

SPAN (Single Parent Action Network)

SPAN provides a nurturing environment for single parents and their children in an atmosphere that is conducive to healing. Community meetings, support groups, and individual counseling are some of its activities.

Families in Step

Stepparents and children share their experiences, learning along the way how to blend two families and build a healthy present and future while understanding the past.

Sibling Project

Children-at-risk who are moving from puberty to adolescence and from elementary to middle or junior high school become part of a support network in an attempt to reduce the social, emotional, and educational stresses encountered during this difficult time of life.

Family Support Program

This program provides follow-up monitoring of developmentally disabled clients previously placed in group homes or residential schools. A broad range of support services for the siblings and parents of these youngsters is an important aspect of the service.

CVacts (Crime Victims' Advocacy, Consultation, Therapy and Support)

Support groups for the parents, siblings, and spouses of murder victims, providing emotional support, sharing experiences regarding the criminal justice system, developing effective means to negotiate bureaucratic systems and advocating for victim's rights.

The Family Bereavement and Recovery Network

Providing support services and opportunities for sharing experiences of bereavement, this program has developed community education and outreach activities which include collaboration with churches and other places of worship, libraries, and funeral homes, all aimed at intervening at a crisis point in individual's lives.

Hispanic Family Life Project

The Hispanic Family Life Project provides an array of services to Hispanic families in order to help them with the process of adaptation to a new country. Outreach, advocacy, and information and referral and clinical services combine with leisure time activities which focus on group and leadership building skills, all aimed at helping youth, especially, to develop strong coping mechanisms. All services provided at the Center are available in Spanish.

APPENDIX II:
CLINIC GROUPS IN AGENCY

Women's Group	6
Single Women's Group	5
Men's Group	3
Mother's Group	1
Marital Group	2
Step-Families Group	3
Young Adults Group	2
Abused Women Group	1
A.P.T.* Women (Incest and Abuse)	2
Parents of Adolescents	4
Parents of Latency Group	3
Parents of Learning Disabled Children	2
Perpetrators Group	1
Learning Disabled Boys Group	2
A.P.T.* Girls (Incest) Group	1
Latency Children of Divorce	4
Adolescent Girls Group	3
Adolescent Boys Group	3
Early Adolescent Girls of Divorce	1
Latency Boys Group	6
Mixed Adolescents	4
Adolescent Boys of Divorce	1
Parents of Developmentally Disabled	1
Mother/Child of Divorce	1
Early Childhood Parents	1
Adult Children of Alcoholics	1
Spouses of Alcoholics	1

*A.P.T. (Abuse Prevention and Treatment)

APPENDIX III

North Shore Child and Family Guidance Center organizes itself around a group participation model in every facet of its functioning. Thus, at the Board, staff and community levels, appropriate individuals are asked to become part of the planning, decision-making and implementation process. The Board, of course, has the usual kinds of committees, i.e., Executive, Budget and Finance, Development, Long Range Planning, etc. In addition, each Family Life project has an Advisory Group which is a mix of Board, Staff, consumers and interested community members at large or from other systems.

The Staff is organized not only into clinical discussion groups (group supervision), but into task-oriented (i.e., administrative) and planning (i.e., project development, staff training and development) groups, as well as a staff relations group to discuss general issues and problems. All input from groups is conveyed to Clinic Committee (representative of all divisions of the Agency) and used for continuance of the planning and implementation process.

Communication is circular; opportunities for leadership are provided both horizontally and vertically in the structure. Our aim is for a sense of ownership in decision-making. External forces impose regulations and restrictions that frustrate us all, and which can make us feel powerless. To counter the impact of bureaucratic control and the kind of alienation that results from the tyranny of paper, we emphasize personal interaction and attempt to provide a sense of attachment and caring. To whatever degree we reach our goal, our clients benefit — for the vision of where we'd like to be is ever-present.

The Black Experience in Suburbia: Prospects and Possibilities for Group Work Intervention

Hugh A. Wilson

SUMMARY. This article seeks to analyze the black experience and status within the suburbs, to offer suggestions around a few areas where group work might prove helpful, and to issue some cautionary notes on the use of group work among black suburbanites.

INTRODUCTION

The modern American suburb, a sprawling nuclear-family based, auto-culture, grew out of a convergence of public policies, private needs, and modern technology after World War II. The marriage boom among returning veterans and the resultant baby boom and severe housing shortages in the cities, the easy availability of the car, the invention of the shopping mall and refrigerated trucks, and the mass production of housing, all contributed greatly to the growth of suburbia (Wattel, 1958; Schnore, 1958; Checkoway, 1980).

But it was explicit governmental policy that made it possible for modern suburbia to exist. By encouraging homeownership and by providing low-interest FHA and VA loans and mortgages, the federal government subsidized the escape of housing-deprived families in the cities to the surrounding suburbs. Federally subsidized highways allowed suburbanites to live farther and farther away from their work places and allowed urban industry and corporations to

Hugh A. Wilson, MSW, is Associate Professor, Department of Political Studies and Director, Institute for Suburban Studies, Adelphi University, Garden City, NY 11530.

relocate in the suburbs (Checkoway, 1980). These post-war policies have led inevitably to America's recreation as a suburban nation. As of 1980, almost half of all Americans resided in suburbs (45%) compared with thirty percent of non-metropolitan areas and twenty five percent in central cities (U.S. Census, 1981).

While America was being suburbanized, however, blacks were severely restricted in their attempts to take full advantage of suburban housing opportunities by explicit federal housing policies — denial of FHA mortgages to black families — and by extensive concerted private discrimination — racial covenants, deed restrictions, and racial steering (Abrams, 1966; Abrams, 1965). These collusive policies between the public and private sectors were responsible for creating and maintaining segregated residential patterns in American suburbs.

This article seeks to analyze the black experience and status within this segregated setting, to offer suggestions around a few areas where group work might prove helpful, and to issue some cautionary notes on the use of group work among black suburbanites.

BLACKS IN THE SUBURBS

The suburbs have been characterized as enclaves for those who hold familistic values i.e., child-centeredness, marriage-centeredness, and a belief that suburbia is a more appropriate place to raise a family and educate children than central cities (Bell, 1958; Mowrer, 1956; Wilson, 1989). Blacks, like whites who move to suburbia, tend to be well-educated, to be upwardly mobile, and to hold high status jobs (Nelson, 1980; Wilson, 1979). And blacks like whites, experience the ongoing delights, diversions, and despair of suburban living: low density single family homes, auto-commutation, shopping malls, increasing property taxes, and fragmented governmental systems.

But while black families and white families with similar socioeconomic backgrounds move to the suburbs for the same reasons, their destinations within suburbia are different. While white families experience social dispersal, within the limitations of income and personal preferences, black families experience reghettoization

as the segregated patterns which existed in central cities are repli-
cated in the suburbs (Connolly, 1973; Stahura, 1988; Clay, 1979).
While in suburbia, black status also undergoes more dramatic
changes than does white status, thus creating a different set of experiences for black families. To highlight these changes and experiences, we look at the patterns of black status in Nassau County, a
typical suburban county outside of New York City.

Blacks in Nassau County

Although Nassau County remains a predominantly white suburban county, blacks have increased their share of the population
from 4.6% in 1970 to 6.8% in 1980. This increase resulted from an
11% decline in the white population and a 37% increase in the black
population (U.S. Census, 1971, Table 34; U.S. Census, 1983, Table 58). As occurs in American suburbs in general, blacks in Nassau County live in largely segregated communities. A study by the
Long Island Regional Planning Board found that eighty two percent
of Nassau's black population resides in ten percent of Nassau's census tracts (Smothers, 1986: p. B2).

There are two major models of black suburban growth: parallel
growth wherein the black and white communities are both growing,
but not at the expense of each other (Farley, 1976) and invasion and
succession[1] where black growth is at the expense of white growth
due to white flight (Stahura, 1988; Massey, 1987). Nassau's black
suburban growth came about through invasion and succession
(Connolly, 1973; Massey, 1987) as white Nassau residents resisted
interracial residential growth by fleeing. For some blacks, this
flight is met with confusion or bitterness. For some blacks, however, white flight is seen as positive. For example, one important
black leader in Nassau County, some years ago, confided to the
author that he welcomed white flight since it opened up housing
possibilities for middle class blacks, and not inconsequentially, provided voters for his power base in his patron-client relationship with
Nassau's white political establishment.[2]

Because blacks came in the second wave of suburbanization,
rather than the first wave, their housing choices were limited. Despite the strong homeowning drive among black suburbanites, only

57% of black householders in Nassau County are homeowners, compared to 81% of white householders (U.S. Census, 1982a: Table 46). Due to racial discrimination, black families tend to depend on the second generation of housing stock, rather than on newly constructed housing for homeownership. This very often leads to black families living in homes that are older and of lower value than those of white homeowners (U.S. Census, 1982a: Table 46). Living in older suburban housing, sometimes necessitates home improvement loans from banking institutions that are less sympathetic to black family aspirations. The result could be increasing economic and social strains on the black suburban family.

Coming in the second wave has also impacted on the demographic character of the black family in Nassau County. While the white population is aging (to be sure there are *some* infusions of young white families) the black population is in the young fertile stage of their life cycle. The median age of blacks in Nassau County in 1980 was 26 years compared to 34.9 years for whites (U.S. Census 1983: Table 182). This younger fertile black population has, of course, resulted in black families having larger households (3.49 persons) than white families (3.04 persons) (U.S. Census, 1983: Table 182). And as could be expected, a larger percentage of the black population is 19 years or younger — 41% — compared to the white population — 28% (U.S. Census, 1983: Table 182).

Black marital status also varies considerably from white marital status. Whereas sixty one percent of whites in Nassau were married, as of 1980, only forty two percent of blacks held that status. The large number of black youth partially accounts for this difference, but there is another factor of some importance contributing to this imbalance. Blacks in Nassau County have substantially higher divorce and separation patterns than whites. For example, whereas five percent of white women were either divorced or separated, thirteen percent of blacks were. (U.S. Census, 1982 b: Table 49).

The higher divorce and separation rates for black families have led to higher rates of female headed households than whites. Whereas one in every twelve white families are headed by women, one in every three black families is headed by a woman (U.S. Census, 1983: Table 183). Thus, black children run a greater risk than white children in growing up in a female headed household in Nassau County. The problem here is not primarily one of economics, as only one third of female headed black families in Nassau County live below the poverty line (U.S. Census, 1983: Table 187).³ This is due to the high education status of black women in Nassau County and their extensive involvement in the labor force. The problem is largely one of appropriate surrogates and services for children while mothers are away at work.

These high separation and divorce rates among black suburban families are probably due, in part, to the social isolation engendered by segregation patterns, the ongoing strain attendant upon a permanent two-income family (see below), and disillusionment with the hollowness of the suburban dream for blacks. These factors might exacerbate normal intra-family tensions to the point where dissolution of the marriage is the only feasible alternative. Thus, it is not that blacks in suburbia are less maritally inclined than whites, but just that the marriages of the former undergo significant additional strains not undergone by the latter. For some black youth in suburbia, the concern here is with their perceptions of marriage as difficult, tension-filled, and disillusioning. Perceptions that might color their future actions around the institution of marriage.

Black median family income is 72% of white family income in Nassau County (U.S. Census, 1983: Table 186). And this despite similar education levels between blacks and whites in Nassau and the disproportionate labor force participation rate of married black women—71%—to married white women—45% (U.S. Census, 1983: Table 184). Even more striking is the divergence in labor force participation rates for black married women and white married women with children under six years, 67% and 24% respectively. (U.S. Census, 1983: Table 184). For black women in Nassau County, working is a necessity as well as a liberating force.⁴ Most black families could not have made the suburban move without two incomes, and cannot maintain a comfortable existence without dual incomes. Although most black families in Nassau are economically comfortable (O'Hare, 1986; Weintraub and Wilson, 1985), fifteen percent of black families live below the poverty level compared to three percent for white families (U.S. Census, 1983: Table 187).

Just as their power around social dispersal is limited, blacks also face limitations in their political power in villages, towns, and school districts in Nassau County. Where they are numerical minorities in villages and in school districts, they exercise minimal power over decision-making. (The author has spent over twenty years as an organizer, trainer, and consultant to community based groups, civil rights groups, and school-based organizations in Nassau County. And during this time there has been consistent resistance to attempts by black groups to share in political and programmatic resources with the notable exception of youth programs and drug programs.) Where blacks are generally a numerical majority, they are usually located in unincorporated areas which have no zoning or taxing powers. Although black suburbanites do control one village and two school districts, they are communities with declining tax bases and large percentages of high risk residents. At the town level blacks are disenfranchised by the system of at-large elections which dilute their population concentrations (Chambers, 1988). One can, with some justification, state that in many communities, blacks have no *social contract* with the various political entities.

The above data indicate that black experiences vary from white experiences in suburbia in the areas of homeownership, spatial patterns, marital status, and life cycle stages. The next section will address the possibilities of group work intervention in these areas.

IMPLICATIONS FOR GROUP WORK

If we interpret group work's various functions as empowerment rather than enabling, as change-oriented rather than adjustment oriented, as community-centered rather than agency centered (Levinson, 1973; Weiss and Ephross, 1986; Breton, 1989; Glassman and Kates, 1986) then group work has a vital role to play in the life of black suburbanites. Towards that end we will look at some of the areas that group work can be pivotal as well as issue some cautionary notes on working with and understanding the black experience.[5]

There appear to be four areas that offer opportunities for group work intervention among blacks in suburbia. The large percentage of blacks under 19 years of age, the large number of children growing up in black female headed households (albeit mostly comfortably) and the large labor force participation rates of black mothers, would seem to indicate that concentration on black suburban youth would be obvious. Intervention in this age group could involve issues around parenting, school advocacy, and community youth facilities. A second area of concern that might be responsive to group work strategies would revolve around the marital status of black suburbanites. This would involve the activation of groups around stabilizing marriages or in dealing with failed or failing marriages. The concern here, of course, is empowering people whether they are within marriages or are single parents.

A third area that seems to invite group work intervention would be the environmental issues that determine, in large part, the black experience in suburbia i.e., discrimination and segregation. Group work might be helpful in the early stages of white flight by mobilizing resources, institutions, and people of good will towards stabilizing communities and halting the seeming inevitability of invasion and succession. Fourth, for those situations where segregation is a reality, group work could aid black suburbanites more effectively mobilizing themselves to influence or control community and political institutions. A major concern here should be the educational system which still largely functions on a daily timetable which presumes a homemaker wife, and which is not overly sympathetic to black values and experiences which differ from mainstream values (see below).

Cautionary Notes

The first and most important cautionary note for the group worker addressing black families is the understanding that *race is the central factor in the black experience* (Robinson, 1989; Report of the National Advisory Commission on Civil Disorders, 1968). The replication of urban segregation patterns in suburbia very often is a blow to black families who have paid their dues and have seemingly attained the American Dream with the suburban move. However, one must be careful not to rush to judgement with concerns about lack of self-esteem here. Despite discrimination and segregation, studies have indicated that there are numerous institutional, community, and kin supports that allow blacks to maintain very positive feelings about themselves (Foster and Perry, 1982; McAdoo, 1981; Powers et al., 1971; Samuels, 1973). The issue is an environmental one not an intra-psychic one.

The group worker should also be attuned to the varigated black experiences in the suburbs. While there is an overarching black reality in suburbia, that reality is very often multi-leveled and multi-hued, affecting different groups of blacks depending on variables such as age, income, family status, stage of the life cycle, education, and ethnicity e.g., Afro-Caribbean or African-American. For example, the problem for wealthy black executives may be the galling inability to secure membership in a country club in order to facilitate business contacts and aid in further upward mobility (Polsky, 1989). For poor suburban black women, the problem might be the widespread lack of prenatal care resulting in infant mortality levels almost three times as high as those of surrounding white suburban communities (Wilson, 1987).

The issue of bi-cultural socialization must also be of paramount importance to group workers in addressing the black experience. Blacks live in a different world than whites, but they must venture into that world for educational, economic, political and other reasons. The result is a dual socialization process with primary socialization occurring within the black world and a secondary socialization occurring within mainstream white society (deAnda, 1984). For those blacks who experience substantial overlap between both cultures, and who utilize an analytical cognitive style, adjustment to mainstream white society is greatly facilitated. However, for those blacks who operate primarily within their own culture, and whose cognitive style is value-bound rather than analytical, adjustment to mainstream society is more difficult (deAnda, 1984). The issue should not be whether analytical or value-bond cognitive styles are correct, but the realization of their existences and the necessity of addressing them in the group work process. In suburbia, it is probable that a substantial portion of black residents, being well-educated and working in the white world, would be more capable of "dealing" with mainstream white values. Poor suburban blacks might more frequently resist or reject mainstream white values.

Growing up in two different societies, blacks and whites not only have different world views and perceptions of institutional legitimacy (Johnson, 1989; Harris and Williams, 1986) but different verbal styles, interactive modes, body languages, and values (McNeely and Badami, 1984; Lum, 1982). A non-black group leader, aware of these differences, will at least ensure that group failure will not occur because of cultural ignorance or arrogance.

Finally, the group worker must be attuned to one of the major conflicts between mainstream white values and black values. Mainstream values, especially under the Reagan Administration, stressed individuality and market place solutions (Moynihan, 1986; Lekachman, 1982) while African-American values stress collective responsibility and governmental solutions (Stack, 1974; McAdoo, 1981; Harris and Williams, 1986). In a suburban setting which stresses the family and non-redistributive allocation of resources, the group worker must challenge suburban values by stressing collectivist values as a means of empowering black suburbanites.

CONCLUSION

The black experience in suburbia, while possessing superficial or surface similarities to that of whites, varies greatly in substantive ways. These variations spring from, or are exacerbated by, the centrality of racial segregation in the lives of black suburban families. Group work has an important role to play in addressing the concerns of black suburbanites by concentrating on empowerment rather than treatment, change rather than adjustment, collectivity rather than individuality.

NOTES

1. It is rather significant that sociologists have used military terms to describe this spatial process.

2. A patron-client relationship stresses political dependency rather than political independency.

3. Comparable figures for white females: 15% in Nassau. A comparable figure for urban blacks: 54% in Manhattan.

4. Some studies indicate that black middle class marriages are more egalitarian than comparable white marriages. Part of this has been attributed to the extensive involvement of black women in the labor force (Axelson, 1970; Landry and Jendrek, 1978).

5. We are concerned here, not with group work techniques, but with potential

areas of interest of intervention as well as detailing some minefields in the interaction between the group worker and black groups.

REFERENCES

Abrams, Charles. *The City is the Frontier*. N.Y.: Harper and Row, 1965.

Abrams, Charles. "The Housing Problem and the Negro," *Daedalus* 95: 64-76.

Bell, Wendell. "Social Choice, Life Styles and Suburban Residence," in William Dobriner (ed.) *The Suburban Community*. N.Y.: Putnam and Sons, 1958. pp. 225-247.

Breton, Margot. "Liberation Theology, Group Work, and the Right of the Poor and Oppressed to Participate in the Life of the Community," *Social Work With Groups* 12, 1989: 5-18.

Chambers, Julius. "Making Hempstead's Black Votes County," *Newsday* Viewpoints Section, September 30, 1988, p. 97.

Checkoway, Barry. "Large Builders, Federal Housing Programs and Postwar Suburbanization," *International Journal of Urban and Regional Research* 4 (March 1980): 21-45.

Clay, Phillip L. "The Process of Black Suburbanization," *Urban Affairs Quarterly* 14 (June 1979): 405-424.

Connolly, Harold X. "Black Movement into the Suburbs," *Urban Affairs Quarterly* 9 (September 1973): 91-111.

deAnda, Diane. "Bicultural Socialization: Factors Affecting the Minority Experience," *Social Work* 29 (March-April 1984): 101-107.

Farley, Reynolds. "The Changing Distribution of Negroes Within Metropolitan Areas: The Emergence of Black Suburbs," in Robert T. Ernst and Lawrence Hugg (ed.) *Black America: Geographic Perspectives* N.Y.: Doubleday, 1976. pp. 333-351.

Foster, Madison and Lorraine K. Perry, "Self-valuation Among Blacks," *Social Work* 27 (January 1982): 60-66.

Glassman, Urania and Len Kates. "Techniques of Social Group Work: A Framework for Practice," *Social Work With Groups* 9 (Spring 1986): 9-38.

Handlin, Oscar. "Motives for Negro Migration to the Suburbs," in *The Newcomers* N.Y.: Doubleday Anchor, 1962. pp. 125-130.

Harris, Frederick and Linda Williams. "JCPS/Gallup Poll Reflects Changing Views on Political Issues," *Focus* 14 (October 1986): 3-4.

Johnson, Julie. "Blacks and Whites are Found 'Worlds Apart,' " *New York Times* January 12, 1989, p. A18.

Landry, Bart and Margaret Platt Jendrek. "The Employment of Wives in Middle Class Black Families," *Journal of Marriage and the Family* 40 (November 1978): 787-797.

Lekachman, Robert. *Greed is Not Enough* N.Y.: Pantheon Books, 1982.

Levinson, Helen M. "Use and Misuse of Groups," *Social Work* 18 (January 1973): 66-73.

McAdoo, Harriette Pipes. "Patterns of Upward Mobility in Black Families," in Harriette Pipes McAdoo (ed.) *Black Families* Beverly Hills: Sage Publications, 1981. pp. 155-169.

McNeely, R.L. and Mary Kenny Badami, "Interracial Communication in School Social Work," *Social Work* 29 (January-February 1984): 22-26.

Mowrer, Ernest R. "The Family in Suburbia," in William Dobriner (ed.) *The Suburban Community* N.Y.: Putnam and Sons, 1958. pp. 147-164.

Moynihan, Daniel Patrick. *Family and Nation* N.Y.: Harcourt Brace Jovanovich, 1986.

Nelson, Kathryn. "Recent Suburbanization of Blacks: How Much, Who, And Where," *Journal of the American Planning Association* 46 (July 1980): 287-300.

New York Times, March 13, 1989. p. B1 and B2.

O'Hare, William. "The Best Metros for Blacks," *American Demographics* 8 (July 1986): 27-29 and 32-33.

Polsky, Carol. "For (White) Members Only", *Newsday* Part 2, July 10, 1989, pp. 4, 5, 10.

Powers, Jerry et al. "A Research Note on the Self-Perception of Youth," *American Educational Research Journal* 8 (November 1971): 665-670.

Report of the National Advisory Commission on Civil Disorders N.Y.: Bantam Books, 1968.

Robinson, Jeanne B. "Clinical Treatment of Black Families: Issues and Strategies," *Social Work* 34 (July 1989); 323-329.

Samuels, Shirley. "An Investigation into the Self-Concepts of Lower and Middle Class Black and White Kindergarten Children," *Journal of Negro Education* 42 (Fall 1973); 467-472.

Schnore, Leo F. "The Growth of Metropolitan Suburbs," in William Dobriner (ed.) *The Suburban Community* N.Y.; Putnam and Sons, 1958. pp. 26-44.

Smothers, Ronald. "For L.I. Blacks Prosperity is a Relative Term," *New York Times* August 1, 1986, pp. B1 & B2.

Stahura, John M. "Changing Patterns of Suburban Racial Composition, 1970-1980," *Urban Affairs Quarterly* 23 (March 1988); 448-460.

Stack, Carol B. *All Our Kin: Strategies for Black Survival in a Black Community* N.Y.: Harper and Row, 1974.

U.S. Bureau of the Census. "U.S. Census of Population: 1970" *General Population Characteristics* Final Report PC (1)B34, New York Washington, D.C.: Government Printing Office, 1971.

U.S. Bureau of the Census. "1980 Census of Population" (Supplementary Reports) *Standard Metropolitan Statistical Areas and Standard Consolidated Areas* Washington, D.C.: Government Printing Office, 1981.

U.S. Bureau of the Census. "Census of Housing" *General Housing Characteristics* V. 1 Part 34 New York HC 801-1-A34 Washington, D.C.: Government Printing Office, 1982a.

U.S. Bureau of the Census, "U.S. Census of Population: 1980: *General Popula-*

tion Characteristics Part 35 New York PC 80-1-B34 Washington, D.C.: Government Printing Office, 1982b.

U.S. Bureau of the Census. "1980 Census of Population, Characteristics of the Population," *General Social and Economic Characteristics* V 1 & 2 Part 34 PC 80-1-C34 Washington, D.C.: Government Printing Office, 1983.

Wattel, Harold. "Levittown: A Suburban Community," in William Dobriner (ed.) *The Suburban Community* N.Y.: Putnam and Sons, 1958. pp. 287-313.

Weintraub, Leta K. and Hugh A. Wilson. *Suburban Distress Index* Garden City, N.Y.: Institute for Suburban Studies, Adelphi University, 1985.

Weiss, Joan C. and Paul H. Ephross. "Group Work Approaches to 'Hate Violence' Incidents," *Social Work* 31 (March-April 1986): 132-136.

Wilson, Hugh. "Getting it on With the Dream," *New York Affairs* 5 (1979): 66-77.

Wilson, Hugh A. "Children in Poverty: The Nassau County Experience" Keynote Address, Annual Luncheon, Nassau Chapter of the National Association of Social Workers, May 8, 1987.

Wilson, Hugh A. "The Family in Suburbia: From Tradition to Pluralism," in Barbara M. Kelly (ed.) *Suburbia Re-examined* N.Y.: Greenwood Press, 1989. pp. 85-93.

Group Work as a Protective Factor for Immigrant Youth

José López

SUMMARY. While constructing a cultural understanding of the adaptation process of Hispanic immigrant youth, this article illustrates how social group process acts as a "protective factor" which promotes a capacity for competence and mastery over their new environment.

PREFACE – THE VISION

As a pre-school aged child I must have heard the letters that my father had written being read aloud. After absorbing these letters, my child's mind conjured up a vision about America. The image was that of an "Infinite white blanket of snow which led to a cathedral."

The peaceful childhood vision of this "white blanket" was transformed into reality when we landed. As I stepped off the plane I was greeted by a great whirling snow storm that whipped up against my cheeks.

Having come from Cuba's tropical climate, I was unprepared for the harsh winter. I had no winter coat, no warm hat, no gloves, no boots and no scarf. It seems like I spent the remainder of my childhood fighting off colds and the flu and well, much more. Beyond the brutal realization that "the blanket" offered no warmth, the sound of a strange language heightened the chill. It was clear then how different I felt and how different everything was. To others I

José López, CSW, is Coordinator of the Hispanic Family Life Project of the North Shore Child and Family Guidance Center, Roslyn Heights, NY 11577. He is interested in formulating models of intervention which assist youth and their families through the adaptation and acculturation process.

spoke another language, one that they did not understand. I did not
eat their food nor dress like them. I had not realized until then that I
had been "left out in the cold."

INTRODUCTION

The term Hispanic is a generic classification of Latin Americans
who share a common language — Spanish. Hispanics come from all
over the world, but mainly Central America, Mexico, the Caribbean, South America and Europe. They share many similar cultural
characteristics stemming from a Spanish and African background,
but have a diverse and rich particular cultural framework. The purpose of this article is to explore the use of group in enabling immigrant Hispanic youth in their struggle to adapt to life in the new
world. Particular emphasis will be placed on an understanding of
the role of group work as a "protective factor" in enhancing resilience and environmental competence and helping the youth to reconcile "old world" and "new world" values.

LA SALIDA: DE PUEBLO A GHETTO, THE DREAM AND REALITY

The dream of coming to the "Golden Land of Opportunity" has
been the driving force behind why people from all over the world
have sought refuge in emigrating to the United States of America.
The dream may be based on the search for political, economic or
religious freedom. While maintaining the extended family kinship
system, large segments of villages ranging from the Caribbean to
the mountain sides of Central America have come to be relocated in
distinct pockets of suburbia (i.e., Long Island, New York). In
America, however, areas like these are known as ghettos or barrios.
Life as it had been in the "pueblo" with a sense of community and
kinship was now transformed into a constant drive for survival.
Stopping by one's "vecino" (neighbor) is no longer acceptable.
Families come here in parts. Perhaps mother may come first and
years later the children arrive. Father may never make it here. Seeking warmth, and a sense of belonging, families huddle together.

Impoverished substandard housing conditions and closed economic opportunities dominate their external reality. Families come to rooms, "compartments" that may be divided by sheets hung from ceilings offering only the semblance of privacy. In Nassau County, a suburb of New York City, according to the most recent statistics, there are currently 58,000 Hispanics. In addition, there are an estimated 60,000 undocumented people (Puerto Rican/Hispanic Legislative Task Force, N.Y. Assembly, March, 1990).

There are basic expectations that most of these families come with: To have a decent affordable place to live, to be employed and to provide educational opportunities for their children . . . dreams that are often deferred. A poem written by Langston Hughes, questions what might happen to a dream deferred:

> What happens to a dream deferred?
> Does it dry up
> Like a raisin in the sun?
> Or fester like a sore —
> and then run?
> Does it stink like rotten meat?
> Or crust and sugar over
> Like a syrupy sweet?
> Maybe it just sags
> Like a heavy load.
> Or does it explode?

Most first generation immigrant families are faced with having to defer their dreams and expectations. The drive for Hispanic youth is often toward adaptation and acculturation as they attempt to separate from their parents. The parents confront their loss of control by maintaining strict cultural values. These factors often alienate Hispanic youth from their families and their culture. While their need to adjust to their new home serves as an adaptive process, they may lose their parents' protection. The pervasive sense of loss generates feelings of helplessness from both generations.

OLD WORLD AND NEW WORLD VALUES COLLIDE

For immigrant Hispanic youth the normal developmental challenges of identity formation and separation/individuation are compounded by family values of loyalty and allegiance. These values are intensified upon settling in the new land.

They conflict with the behavioral style of many of their American contemporaries who may be strident in the areas of self expression and the establishment of a unique identity (i.e., clothes, language, style, etc.). This is further compounded by the loss of expectations. The new country's "unlimited opportunities" become tempered with the realities of having to adapt to a new culture, a new language and a new educational system, acquiring legal citizenship and fighting for economic survival. One of the purposes of the group to be described herein is to reconcile the values of the two worlds.

DISLOCATION AND LOSS

Oliva M. Espina, who has written about the psychological impact of historical dislocation explains:

> Studies of learned helplessness demonstrated that when individuals find themselves trapped in situations they cannot control, they tend to become seriously depressed. . . . the most immediate feeling experienced after leaving such a situation of danger is relief . . . together with sadness and grief for those left behind. Confusion and frustration about all the new places and people and customs encountered soon add further burdens. (5)

On a personal level, she recalls her own plight:

> there were things I shared with them, however, that I cannot share now with my close friends in the United States. No matter how fluent I am in English, my innermost feelings are in Spanish, and my poetry is only in Spanish. This deepest part of myself remains hidden from people who are extremely important for me, no matter how hard we all try. I can translate,

but translated feelings like translated poetry are just not the same. (5.P.5/7)

As all familiarity with an external environment vanishes an emotional upheaval occurs evoking excitement, fascination, terror, fantasy and loss. Hopes and aspirations collide with inescapable realities which become roadblocks to dreams of a new life. These obstacles can appear insurmountable generating a sense of helplessness and loss of coherent vision of the future. All energy is devoted to survival. In discussing the complexity involved in negotiating external forces, Harry Aponte notes:

> The rapidity of technological and social changes is greater today that at any previous period in human history . . . A major reason for this progressive acceleration of social change is the explosion in the amount and quality of information through schools, the media, telephones, computers, and more accessible travel. It has played a prime role in escalating the rate of change of traditional relationships between races, socioeconomic groups, age groups, the sexes and other social networks . . . Walls collapse and options multiply. Traditions, customs and roles within social relationships are forced to contend with mounting pressure to change. They resist, accommodate, mutate, or vanish within the swirl of social movement. (3.P.21)

Placing this whirlwind of change within the context of being ripped from your homeland, community and family serves to further the loss of control, bewilderment and helplessness. Many Hispanic parents sadly observe the "Americanization" of their children as they attempt to separate and to belong by experimenting with many of the dominant culture's values. For many, the higher the level of adaptation and acculturation to mainstream, the greater the distance from the family of origin.

PROTECTIVE FACTORS: TIES THAT BIND

Emmy Werner, amongst others, identified "protective factors" associated with promoting resilience in youth. These protective factors are based on a range of systems functioning together: Constitu-

tional assets such as "dispositional attributes, activity level and so-
ciability, intelligence, expressive language skills and an internal
locus of control; affectional ties within the family that provide emotional support in times of stress, whether from a parent, sibling,
spouse, or mate; and external support systems (environment)
whether in school, at work, or church that reward the individual's
competencies and determination and provide a belief system by
which to live (23.P.80). The group to be discussed herein incorporates the concept of the "therapeutic group contribution" as a protective factor in helping Hispanic youth develop positive adaptive
behaviors to the acculturation process (summarized in Appendix I).
As a therapeutic tool, the group provides support, acceptance, encouragement and validation. While immigrant youth are adapting
they suffer from loss of self esteem. The group fosters self esteem
and encourages self expression and positive attitudes toward goal
achievement and educational attainment. It serves as a form to facilitate communication and promote self acceptance. The group provides an avenue through which networks can be developed and
maintained, protective elements once provided by the extended
family kinship system.

GROUP FORMATION: FINDING A PLACE

You have to help your father because he is your father. . . .
you know.

These are the words of a fifteen year old Dominican girl who was
describing her plight in translating for her disabled father, in a com-
pensation hearing room. He had been disabled for a year and a half
after seriously injuring himself carrying cement bags.
This young adolescent girl was one of fifteen to twenty youth
who came together weekly in a suburban high school on the affluent
north shore of Long Island, New York. They were between the ages
of fifteen to eighteen. The group was formed by offering an invitation to anyone wishing to participate to attend. Meetings were held
in the school's conference room. It should be noted that there had
been numerous complaints about the behaviors of many of the Hispanic students by school personnel. The group composition in-

cluded a mixture of boys and girls from virtually all parts of the Caribbean, South America and war torn regions of Central America. There was also a range of years to months that the students had been in the United States.

Issues related to feelings of inclusion and exclusion predominated the early group meetings. The members debated about what language to speak and about which national ethnic group was more "together." They struggled over whether or not to allow others to join the group.

The more studious members were criticized by some for becoming too "Americanized" while others bragged about cutting classes or failing tests. Although many of these discussions, rooted in internal conflict about acculturation, stimulated a variety of opinions there was one area of clear consensus. The group felt persecuted by school personnel, whom they alleged didn't provide a place for them.

> The Jews have a place; the blacks have a place; the jocks have a place, the greasers have a place, the burnouts have a place, the orientals have a place . . . What do we have? We can't even hang out in the hallway.

The role of the worker,* the author, was somewhat precarious as the tacit directive from the school's administration was to keep the peace — "quiet the group down." Feelings of "being an outsider" helped the worker to empathize with the group. These feelings were reinforced on numerous occasions when the group's "room" was locked! The members were locked out and left wandering the halls in search of someone to open the door.

The worker's role, to paraphrase William Schwartz, was to "help the group and the school rediscover their stake in one another." Through discussion, planning, advocacy and negotiation the group eventually got their place within the school walls and they began to feel empowered. In the aftermath of securing a special place the need to discover an even greater space emerged, a space

---

*The worker came to the school via his agency, a community mental health clinic (North Shore Child and Family Guidance Center). The work described is one of many outreach efforts to local school districts in the area.

beyond the school walls, beyond their day to day environment. Out of this, the worker offered the opportunity for the group to organize a trip.

EARLY PLANNING:
MEMORIES AND POSSIBILITIES

The introduction of the opportunity to plan a trip elicited fantasies of being out in open fields, simply running and jumping. Memories of their homelands, swimming in rivers and of catching wild birds were juxtaposed with the limitations of where and when they could go. Funds were needed. Lost memories collided with stark realities. What followed was a series of events, planning a new trip that perhaps symbolized the reconstruction of their original trip to America. What was different now was that this trip was to be to an open, green and safe place. This old place in New York was "Bear Mountain." Bear Mountain offered of course, mountains, swimming and plenty of open green fields. As a bonus it even had a small zoo.

As the group evolved, the support system formed by the group was akin to the extended family system and became the source through which the group organized. As trust developed they were able to share emotional conflicts they were experiencing. Having successfully secured a place in the school, the group shifted from an extra familial (societal) to a familial frame of reference. They expressed their guilt about the problems they gave their mothers and shared stories of broken families and divided loyalties. Carlos, a 14 year old from Mexico, spoke of his father's new liaison and of a half brother he never knew and of his mother's domestic work to support him and his younger brother. They often spoke of the alienation and the sense of exclusion which they always felt. Margo, an extremely bright, verbal, young lady, spoke of her mother's inability to accept her "going out at night." She spoke of her mother's isolation since the death of her father.

As a way of fostering affectional ties through the group, those who were to be attending the trip were directed to extend an invitation to their parents. A goal of the group is to strengthen identity development and to build positive awareness of psycho-cultural differences. By inviting their parents intergenerational differences could be bridged. The group initially resisted this idea. They felt that the parents would hamper their style, inhibit their expressive behavior and ultimately embarrass them. After some consideration, however, they agreed. Parents were to be active only in the supervision of the trip. It was interesting to note how ineffective they envisioned their parents to be. They no longer felt that they needed their protection. Perhaps they felt they had been without it for too long.

THE TRIP: A CALL FOR ACTION

Melvin Delgado, describing the use of activities in group work with Hispanic youth, notes the following:

> The worker should foster a value orientation stressing action that requires development of concrete solutions. Group goals should be short rather than long term and easily measurable by the group. A present time orientation stresses current problems and solutions. A group leader, in turn, must refrain from focusing on the past or future. His/her direction should be present-time oriented, helping the group to find solutions that, keeping in tune with a doing orientation, can be implemented. (17. P. 86/87)

The group, confronted with the reality of having to raise funds to rent a bus and buy lunch, organized two successful school dances which raised twelve hundred dollars. The group organized committees and delegated responsibilities. Artists emerged and decorations were made. Tickets to the dance were primarily sold to the main student body. A disc jockey who belonged to both the Hispanic group and the Anglo world volunteered to whirl the records. Since many of the group members were employed after school at various local businesses, they successfully negotiated obtaining donations for missing decorations and food for these dances. The group made a conscious decision that since the majority of the students attending were Anglo, they would not play Latin music. At the end of each dance though, they decided to close with their favorite Latin cut, as if to add their unique signature to each dance.

The worker's role included obtaining the various permits and the paper work needed to process the funds through the school. Many obstacles were put forth by the school administration. These included, obtaining chaperones (teachers to volunteer) that exceeded the ordinary number, allaying the fears of the school personnel that the students would not destroy the building, and agreeing to an ending time that would be reasonable to the young people. The group weathered all obstacles and achieved their goal. The planning and successful production of the dances reinforced a sense of self acceptance, competence and mastery.

The bus for Bear Mountain arrived at 7:30 A.M. for an 8:00 A.M. departure. All, with the exception of three who arrived minutes later, were there. Moving from the coolness of the Manhattan skyline to the mountainsides of New Jersey, one could feel the bus relax. The mood was playful and the mixture of current top disco music and the frenetic merengue filled the air. The bus rocked right on up to Bear Mountain. When the young travellers arrived they resembled little rabbits let loose into the open countryside after having been caged.

As a small group hiked up through a trail, they remembered childhood games "al escondido" (hide and seek), memories of looking for frogs and snakes and how many different types there were. . . . A young man spoke to the worker about his current dilemma of maybe having to drop out of school. They were happy, at least for that day. The parents who participated also seemed to be overwhelmed with the experience of being out in the open, in a different place. They spoke anxiously about getting groups of their friends to come together and on their own and they pressed the worker for directions on how to return. They felt happy that their children were safe, protected by the environment and they were glad to be a part of it.

CONCLUSION

Group processes which encourage self acceptance and validate external realities are critical to the adjustment of individuals and families confronted with migration. The group serves as a protective factor contributing to the positive adaptation of Hispanic/immigrant youth.

As an immigrant who has undergone thirty years of acculturation the worker's awareness of his own frustrations in negotiating outside systems enabled him to tune into the members' sense of helplessness. Beyond this it helped him lend a vision which served to empower the youth with a renewed sense of mastery. Memories and building new bridges helped both worker and group to discover common ground. The "white blanket of snow" became a guide to opening doors and taking a journey to a free and open place.

REFERENCES

Bacznskyj, Wawa, LICSW, "Treating Children and Adolescents, Psychotherapy of Diversity Conference, Harvard Medical School, Boston, Mass., May 1989.

Bernstein, S. Explorations in Group Work. Boston University School of Social Work, 1965.

Comas-Diaz, L. and Griffin, E., Clinical Guidelines in Cross Cultural Mental Health. John Wiley and Sons. New York, 1988.

Davis, L. Guest Ed. "Ethnicity in Social Group Work Practice" in Social Work with Groups. Papell, C. and Rothman, B. Seried Eds., Vol. 7, Number 3. The Haworth Press, New York, Fall 1984.

Espina, O. "Roots Uprooted: Reflections on the Psychological Impact of Historical Dislocation." Tufts University, Massachusetts. 1987.

Farber, A. and Rogler, L. Unitas: Hispanic and Black Children in a Healing Community. Hispanic Research Center, Fordham University, Bronx, New York, 1981.

Flach, F. Resilience: Discovering a New Strength at Times of Stress. Ballantine Books, New York, 1988.

Fitzpatrick, J. Puerto Rican Americans: The Meaning of Migration to the Mainland. Prentice-Hall, Inc., Englewood Cliffs, New Jersey, 1971.

Frank, B., Marel, R. et al. Statewide Household Survey of Substance Abuse, 1986; Illicit Substance Use Among Hispanic Adults in New York State. Bureau of Research and Evaluation, 1988.

Giordano, J. Ed. "Group Identity and Mental Health" in International Journal of Mental Health, Vol. 5, Number 2. International Arts and Sciences Press, Inc. White Plains, New York, Summer, 1976.

Holzman, L., Ed. Practice: The Journal of Politics, Economics, Psychology, Sociology and Culture. Practice Press, New York 1989.

Kleinman, A. "The Illness Narratives: Suffering, Healing and the Human Condition." Basic Books, 1988.

Levine, B. Fundamentals of Group Treatment. Whitehall Co., Northbrook, Illinois, 1967.

Mack, John, E., M.D., "From a Conflict to an Empowerment Model" Psychotherapy of Diversity Conference, Harvard Medical School, Boston Mass., May 1989.

Malekoff, A. "Socializing Pre-Adolescents into the Group Culture" in Social Work with Groups, Kolodny, R. and Garland, J. Guest Eds. Vol. 7, No. 4 Haworth Press, New York, Winter 1984.

McGoldrick, M., Pearce J. and Giordano, J. Eds. Ethnicity and Family Therapy. Guilford Press, New York, 1982.

Middleman, R. Guest Editor. "Activities and Action in Groupwork" in Social Work with Groups, Papell, C. and Rothman, B., Series Eds. Vol. 6, No. 1. Haworth Press, New York, Spring, 1983.

Montiel, M. Hispanic Families: Critical Issues for Policy and Programs in Human Services. COSSMHO, The National Coalition of Hispanic Mental Health and Human Services Organizations, Washington, D.C., 1978.

Rogg, E. and Cooney, R. Adaptation and Adjustment of Cubans: West New York, New Jersey. Hispanic Research Center, Fordham University. Bronx, New York, 1980.

Rogler, L. and Cooney, R. Puerto Rican Families in New York City: Intergenerational Processes. Waterfront Press. Maplewood, New Jersey, 1985.

Shore, M., Ed. American Journal of Orthopsychiatry. Vol. 59, No. 2. New York, April, 1989.

Sissons, P. The Hispanic Experience of Criminal Justice, Monograph No. 3, Hispanic Research Center, Fordham University, Bronx, New York, 1979.

Werner, Emmy, E. High Risk Children in Young Adulthood: A Longitudinal Study from Birth to 32 Years. American J. Orthopsychiatry 59(1), January, 1989.

Zambrana, R., Ed. Work and Family and Health: Latina Women in Transition. Hispanic Research Center, Fordham University, Bronx, New York, 1982.

APPENDIX A. Protective Factors Related to the Adaptation and Acculturation Process of Hispanic/Minority Youth

CONSTITUTIONAL ASSETS	FAMILIAL CONTRIBUTIONS	ENVIRONMENTAL CONTRIBUTIONS	THERAPEUTIC GROUP CONTRIBUTIONS
Capacity to handle change (i.e., aspects of immigration: age, country of origin & circumstances of travel)	Flexibility toward adaptation	Social acceptance, acquisition of appropriate housing, social/educational/vocational support	Listens Supports Accepts Encourages Validates
Cognitive, intellectual endowments	Encouragement toward self development	Provides appropriate educational supports (including language acquisition)	Ego support and role development
Capacity for self-regulation	Allowance for independent functioning with appropriate supervision	Reinforces positive behaviors and fosters competence and competition	Enhances educational experience and fosters self-pride

41

APPENDIX A (continued)

CONSTITUTIONAL ASSETS	FAMILIAL CONTRIBUTIONS	ENVIRONMENTAL CONTRIBUTIONS	THERAPEUTIC GROUP CONTRIBUTIONS
Capacity for future goal orientation and achievement	Ability to facilitate successful separation/ individuation	Provides avenue for educational/vocational achievement and planning	Fosters self-acceptance and encourages competence and mastery
Capacity for relationship development	Recognizes and accepts differences and shifts in life styles	Provides opportunities for multi-cultural experiences	Strengthens identity development and builds positive awareness of psycho-cultural differences
Capacity toward environmental mastery (wherewithal)	Provides support and formulates approaches to solve problems	Provides opportunities for community/school involvement, fostering a sense of empowerment	Provides avenues for network building and sharing of experiences and frustrations

Group Work with Bulimic Adolescent Females in Suburbia

Karen V. Harper
Lee S. Shillito

SUMMARY. Suburban adolescent females live in environments that are competitive, achievement oriented, and appearance centered. Those adolescent girls in suburban populations who are experiencing bulimic symptomatology are often unwilling to seek help because of feelings of shame over their binge-purge behaviors. Bulimic support groups offering education and supportive intervention allow adolescent bulimic girls in suburbia to self-identify, to examine their body misperceptions and beliefs about food, and to seek ways of living that are not centered on weight management.

INTRODUCTION

Adolescent females from middle and upper socioeconomic classes exhibit eating disorders more often than do their peers of lower socioeconomic status (Faust, 1987). Bulimia is an eating disorder characterized by recurrent episodes of binge/eating followed by efforts to undo caloric intake and prevent weight gain through self-induced vomiting, laxative or diuretic ingestion, strict dieting,

Karen V. Harper, PhD, LISW, is Assistant Professor and Lee S. Shillito, LISW, is Research Assistant and a doctoral student, Ohio State University College of Social Work, Columbus, OH 43210.

The support group model presented by Harper and Shillito evolved from their work with middle and upper-middle-class adolescents living in relatively secluded suburbs in central Ohio's major metropolitan area. Most often these suburban areas include single family homes with two parents, approximately one-third of whom are remarried, with two or three children. Generally both parents have college degrees and work outside the home, commute only short distances to jobs, live in spacious houses, and have two or more automobiles.

43

fasting, or vigorous exercise (American Psychiatric Association, 1987). Central to bulimia is a preoccupation with calories, body weight and a phobia about weight gain (Anderson, 1985). Bulimia appears to begin in middle or late adolescence and to continue well into adulthood (Mallick, Whipple and Huerta, 1987). Reports of incidence of this eating disorder vary widely for a population, from 3.8 to 19% (Halmi, Falk & Schwartz, 1981; Pyle et al., 1983; Wermuth et al., 1977; Johnson et al., 1984). One study of 1500 high school youth determined that 6.73% of female students and .20% of male students reported having experienced bulimic behaviors (Howat and Saxton, 1988).

Far too often our society fails to educate its youth about the serious medical consequences of dysfunctional eating patterns. Bulimia can be a life-threatening eating disorder that can lead to such dire physical complications as electrolyte disturbances, cardiac irregularities, kidney dysfunctioning, neurological abnormalities, gastrointestinal disturbances, dental deterioration, swollen salivary glands, edema and dehydration, menstrual irregularities, amenorrhea, and emotional instability aggravated by metabolic abnormalities (Garner et al., 1985; Johnson and Connors, 1987). It has been said that eating disorders begin in adolescence and that teenage girls are subjects for treatment and study (Mallick, Whipple & Huerta, 1987).

Bulimic adolescents have some awareness that their eating behavior is abnormal and often experience shame around their binge/purge behavior that results in an inability to disclose their eating problems to others (Johnson and Connors, 1987). Due to the secrecy of their eating behaviors, bulimics often are not identified. Their failure to identify themselves as needing help is exacerbated by the nature of the search for privacy in daily living and consequential isolation of suburban families (Baldassare, 1986). Therefore, it follows that bulimic adolescents in suburbia run the risk of being hidden from identification and treatment. One means of providing intervention to adolescent bulimic females who are 16+ years of age and who attend suburban high schools is through professional support groups. This article provides a rationale and a model for eight weeks of professional support group treatment for bulimic adolescents in suburbia.

BULIMIA: AN EATING DISORDER
OF ADOLESCENTS

Our society's preoccupation with slimness impacts on young females and how they relate to their bodies and to food intake as they
move through the biopsychosocial phases of adolescent development. Newman and Newman (1987) characterize early/mid adolescence (ages 13 through 17 years of age) by rapid physical changes
and sensitivity to peer approval. During this developmental phase
adolescent girls experience significant changes in shape, height,
and weight as their bodies mature into adulthood. During this accel-
erated growth phase adolescent girls also experience significant
weight gain and an increase of subcutaneous fat (Newman and
Newman, 1987). The physical changes of early/mid adolescence
have psychological importance for girls as they seek membership in
a peer group and as they attempt to be considered attractive by
society in general and by young males in particular. Because society equates thinness with feminine beauty, it follows that a majority
of adolescent girls feel pressured to attain lower body weight in
accordance with their unrealistic perceptions of socially prescribed
beauty (Garner, Garfinkel and Olmsted, 1983).

Adolescent girls, perceiving their developing bodies as over-
weight in comparison to the slender frames promoted by the media
and fashion industries, attempt bodily reduction through restrictive
dieting. Caloric deprivation triggers a biologically determined hunger drive that leads many of these adolescent girls into binge eating
episodes and resulting weight gain. This starving/binging behavior
presents an opportunity for those adolescent females who are most
fat phobic to turn to bulimia as a weight management strategy.

ARE FEMALE ADOLESCENTS IN SUBURBIA
AT RISK FOR BULIMIA?

Decentralization of major urban areas over the past fifty years
produced suburban areas that are populated by middle and upper
income families (Baldassare, 1986). These families live in well
kept homes that often are spacious and expensive. According to
Fishman (1987), the social legacy of suburbia is that there has been

a reduction of those whose inner direction manifests in moral judg-
ment and clear decision making. At the same time there has been an
increase of those who are directed by others through conformity,
compliance and an image of follower rather than leader. In this
environment, adolescents have been assigned to a lengthy social
and economic moratorium where their productivity is unneeded.
These adolescents pursue education and are often directed by parental influence until well into young adulthood. Larkin (1979) pro-
poses that capitalistic development and bourgeois culture have
placed adolescents at risk of identity crisis. Many of these suburban
adolescents search for meaning in their unreal world that is insulated from harsher realities of inner cities and the world at large.

Suburban adolescent girls reared in insulated families that are
frequently enmeshing often lack intergenerational family involvement and/or long-term support systems. Suburban families are typically achievement oriented, status conscious, and appearance sensitive. These families frequently experience economic pressures and
underlying needs such as loneliness and helplessness (Malekoff,
Levin, & Quaglia, 1987). The daughters in these suburban family
constellations are often perfectionistic, particularly in regard to
their physical appearance, and are sensitive to external approval.
Their self-identity may be crippled by their enmeshed upbringing.
These upwardly mobile middle and upper class-conscious families
give mixed messages regarding female behaviors because of their
own ambivalence toward modern day emancipation and traditional
values. Bulimic daughters preoccupied with feminine appearances
are caught in the double bind of achievement versus compliancy.
Daughters in these upwardly mobile families are reported to be so-
cialized to achieve while simultaneously encouraged to be nonas-
sertive and compliant (Schwartz, 1985).

A MODEL FOR PROFESSIONAL SUPPORT GROUPS

Group treatment with bulimic clients has been recognized as an
effective modality for some time (Roth, D. M. & Ross, D. R.,
1988). Although related to treatment, these groups do not have the
explicit goal of "curing" this behavioral problem. Professionally
led support groups have been defined as those groups that are facili-

tated by professionals (Enright, Butterfield and Berkowitz, 1985). Social workers trained in eating disorders and group work are well suited to work with this group of adolescent bulimics (Mintz, 1985). A recovered bulimic who is close in age to the adolescent group members will join the social worker as co-leader. This co-leader must be free of bulimic behaviors for at least one year's duration. The co-leader will share in prescreening and will serve as a role model. Given the resistance which many adolescents often exhibit in the presence of an adult provider, the co-leader has an important responsibility in facilitating communication and establishing trust in the group. The social worker is responsible for membership screening, session content, boundary maintenance and culture building in the group. These functions are important in the instance of bulimic adolescents who may be in a support group for the first time and may just be recognizing that others share the same preoccupation with food and self image.

Objectives for Support Groups for Bulimic Adolescents

The objectives to be accomplished through support groups with bulimic adolescents are:

1. To provide education and information about eating disorders.
2. To provided a supportive experience for identifying and sharing feelings.
3. To facilitate management of eating behaviors.
4. To facilitate development of realistic expectations for self and others.
5. To experience improved interpersonal relationships through reaching out to others.
6. To develop an awareness of self in relation to socio-cultural pressures.

These objectives are based on knowledge of bulimia as a cognitive behavioral disorder rather than a personality disturbance. The most distinctive features of bulimia are dysfunctional beliefs and values concerning body shape and weight (Fairburn, 1985). Bulimics have an irrational fear of fatness (Anderson, 1985) as well as distorted body perceptions that are expressed in binge/purge behaviors (Wooley & Wooley, 1985). ". . . rather than being simply symptomatic of bulimia, these beliefs and values appear to be of primary importance in the maintenance of their condition" (Fairburn 1985, p. 161).

Group Structure

This professionally led support group meets weekly for a total of eight sessions. Eating-disordered adolescents are unlikely to enter this group with a clear understanding of their problems or the extent of bulimia which they may be experiencing. Therefore, a semi-closed structure allows some openness in order to help adolescent bulimics identify their eating problems and determine if they wish to participate in the group. The first week is an open session with the remaining seven sessions being closed. Group sessions are to last 90 minutes. The open group is a means of empowering adolescents to make their own commitment to group membership. After the first session, the group is closed to new members and/or observers. Although attendance is voluntary, members are encouraged to attend and all absences will be followed by one telephone call.

Pre-Group Activities

Employing a prevention model often used by mental health and child welfare providers, recruitment for group membership begins with an educational campaign in suburban high schools. Anorexia and bulimia will be defined as potentially life threatening eating disorders. Educational information can be distributed through literature drops, student assemblies, and school newspapers. Bulletin board posters need to include notices of planned support groups for students who fear being out of control of their weight and who may not be eating for periods of time, eating large quantities of food, vomiting, and using laxatives or diuretics to control weight. Packets with notices of individual conference times, registration blanks, telephone numbers for further information, and a professional registry of counselors, physicians, and nutritionists who specialize in treating eating disorders are to be made available throughout the school.

Pre-screening interviews are to be conducted with self-referring and/or referred females. Each potential group member is to receive information concerning the full range of eating disorders. Through careful pre-screening, those students who are bulimic can be identified and can consider the appropriateness of this group for their needs. Adolescents with apparent personality disturbances, suicidal ideation or anorexia are to be referred for appropriate treatment. The need to have and to give confidentiality to others will be discussed during the prescreening interview. All support groups are to be held after school so that participants are not absent from classes.

CONTENT OF GROUP SESSIONS
FOR BULIMIC ADOLESCENTS

Session #1: The Importance of Food
in Our Lives

Group Session Objective

To provide education and information about eating disorders and to establish rapport and cooperative interaction with and among group members.

Content: After introductions the co-leader reviews ground rules of the eight group sessions including: confidentiality, closed group structure, attendance, meeting place, time, group objectives, and homework assignments. The social work leader provides a thirty-minute presentation concerning the importance of good eating habits. The influence of social pressures to be thin, to excel in school and to be popular are discussed as external stressors. The use of binge eating as a mechanism to reduce stress in personal, social and emotional lives is presented with cartoon transparencies. A video presentation from media advertisements showing images of "slimness as beautiful" demonstrates one way external pressure affects how each person sees herself.

Exercise: Each participant is given a sheet of drawing paper and asked to draw a self-profile as they see themselves and a second profile of how they would like to look. The members are asked to share their pictures with one other person in the group and to talk about their interest and intent to attend the remaining seven sessions.

Homework: Food diaries will be part of weekly homework for all sessions. At the beginning of each session the group leaders will give out packets (containing 7 sheets for 7 days) to group members. Each group member is to complete and maintain a notebook of these daily food records that identify degree of hunger present, food type and quantity consumed, activity while eating, time spent eating, location, eating with whom, feelings while eating and purging methods used. The goal of this exercise is to assist participants in identifying eating responses that occur in response to psychological rather than physical needs.

Session #2: Examining Bulimia: Why Am I a Member of This Group?

Group Session Objective

To encourage group participation through facilitating identification of eating behaviors and alternative stress management options.

Exercise: Group members are welcomed and introductions are repeated. Group rules for the closed structure and confidentiality are reviewed. The co-leader begins the session by facilitating a discussion of food diaries. Participants are asked to share something from their diaries with the group. Discussion time is 30 minutes.

Content: Next, the social worker provides a description of bulimia and the functions served by this behavior. Each participant is provided with a personal and confidential checklist for assessing eating behaviors and potential problems. Discussion about problem solving includes examples of different responses to stress, use of food, and the prevalence of bulimia in populations such as their suburban, achievement oriented community.

Homework: Food diary continues in week two. Group members are asked to replace the urge to binge/purge with a pleasurable activity during the week and to be prepared to share it with the group. Support through the week is encouraged by asking group members to exchange telephone numbers with at least one other person in the group and to make one or more daily telephone calls.

Session #3: Personal, Medical and Social Meanings of Bulimia

Group Session Objective

To provide education about the consequences of bulimia and to identify alternatives to dysfunctional eating.

Exercise: Food diaries for week two are shared. Next, the co-leader facilitates discussion of pleasurable activities that members used to replace eating behaviors during the previous week. Group members are encouraged to share and compare experiences and to generate alternatives to eating behaviors.

Content: This week's presentation concerns the negative consequences of bulimia, including psychological, social and physical deterioration. The body's set point, the biologically determined weight for one's body type, influences how the body makes use of food and reduces metabolism in response to caloric deprivation. Repeated caloric deprivation tends to reduce the amount of calories that the body needs to maintain its weight.

Homework: Food diaries are to continue. Group members will make a collage of pictures of a nutritious day experienced during the week.

Session #4: Healthy Living Through Nutrition

Group Session Objective

To correct misconceptions about nutrition and to develop healthy eating plans that provide for management of eating disorders.

Exercise: Group sharing and discussion of last week's food diaries are extended to include participants' observations of any changes that can be identified from their diary. The group is encouraged to reinforce successes and to suggest ways of managing problems. Homework collages are shared and discussed.

Content: Identification of misconceptions about nutrition is followed by group members sharing their specific food myths. Among these food myths are the convictions that: "Carbohydrates make you fat." "If I only eat one meal a day, I won't get fat." "Laxatives keep me thin." "If I eat one cookie, I have blown my entire diet." Next, a discussion of healthy nutrition includes the importance of the four major food groups in maintaining health and nutritional handbooks providing information on healthy meal planning are given out. Discussion regarding weight management through healthy eating is reviewed through hypothetical meal planning.

Homework: Food diaries continue. Group members collect photos of "How I think I look" and "how I'd like to look."

Session #5: Body Image

Group Session Objective

To examine the discrepancy between perceived and actual body size.

Exercise: Food diaries are shared and discussed. The homework photos of physical and projected images of self are shared with the group. Group members are asked to draw an outline of themselves on a large paper hung on the wall. The members then stand by the paper and co-leader and social worker draw each member's actual body outline. Discussion then centers upon the discrepancy between imaged and real body sizes.

Content: A brief presentation focuses on the importance of correcting negative body image. Negative perception of body size is a common problem for many people, particularly for weight conscious bulimics. Societal pressures, advertisements in the media and pressures from family and friends contribute to how women see themselves.

Homework: Members are to continue food diaries. They are to think about the body outlining exercise during the coming week. What was its meaning for them? What do distorted body images have to do with their lives?

Session 6: Negative Images and Dysfunctional Eating

Group Session Objective

To identify the underlying irrational beliefs and values that support bulimic behaviors.

Exercise: Share and discuss food diaries. The group will discuss last week's body outlining exercise and will work toward understanding how body images formed in response to social and familial pressures.

Content: This week's presentation will address dysfunctional beliefs and values that perpetuate bulimia. Social and familial pressures for slimness will be identified and each member will be provided a worksheet to list strategies to minimize the impact of these messages on eating behaviors.

Homework: Food diaries are to be continued. Each member is to bring two magazine photos with her to the next session. One photo is to answer the question, "How I look?" and the other is to answer, "Who I'd like to look like."

Session #7: Feeding Yourself Emotionally

Group Session Objective

To empower group members to take charge of their social, physical, and emotional well being.

Exercise: Food diaries will be discussed with emphasis being placed on each member identifying individual triggers for bulimic eating behaviors. As magazine photos are shared by the group members, the co-leader will summarize group discussion to provide summary feedback. Feelings about this feedback will be elicited and positively supported.

Content: This session's presentation identifies ways to be emotionally nurturant without abusing food. Discussion will center on self-actualization as a key to emotional and personal strength as well as a key to controlling bulimic behaviors. Taking charge of personal time, involvement with food, communication with friends and family members and participation in recreational activities are essential to being more self-actualized.

Homework: Food diaries are to be continued. In preparation for the final session of the group, members are to collect pictures of different feelings expressed by flowers, happy faces, tears, broken glass, etc.

Session #8: Where to Go from Here?

Group Session Objective

To integrate experiences from the support group sessions.

Exercise: Review food diaries, compare session #1 diary with session #8 and discuss how they are alike and different. Determine if triggers for eating behaviors are the same or different in session #8 than in session #1.

Content: Emphasis is placed upon progress made during the group's involvement for eight weeks. Accomplishments to be reviewed include: an understanding of eating disorders, particularly bulimia; medical and social aspects of bulimia; healthy nutrition; food and body image misconceptions; realistic body imaging; positive feelings and feedback; and the productive use of time and activity.

Exercise: The co-leader will help group members evaluate progress and discuss strengths and limitations in their management of eating behaviors. Exchanging telephone numbers with other group members will provide a lasting support network. A final activity will be group discussion around the benefit of the group. Options for future treatment will be discussed and registries of nurses, doctors, nutritionists, social workers, counselors, nutritionists, etc., will be provided.

DISCUSSION

Social group work is an important method in treating bulimia (Mintz, 1985). Support groups such as the one presented in this article are particularly helpful with adolescent females in suburbia who may be developing misconceptions about the role of food in their lives and/or who may be experiencing bulimic symptomatology. These support groups are mutually empathetic rather than competitive, supportive rather than alienating, and accepting rather than critical. For some of these adolescent females with underlying dysfunctional beliefs and values, bulimia may be a lasting and serious disorder. When used with adolescents who are entering the bulimic syndrome, support groups such as these provide a positive setting in which to identify food and body misconceptions and problematic eating behaviors. Further, support groups may prevent increasingly dysfunctional eating disorders and may help the adolescent develop an openness toward seeking and receiving help. Some will be empowered to not only take charge of their lives and their eating behaviors, but also, to provide help and support to others in experiencing eating disorders.

The structured and focused approach to education and treatment provide support group members with feedback about their thoughts, beliefs, and values that are perpetuating their bulimic behavior. Food diary exercise provides an opportunity for self-observation of eating attitudes and behavior. Affective sharing, mutual support and awareness of perceptual distortions and value misconceptions are important milestones in bulimic intervention.

In conclusion, adolescent females in suburbia who suffer from bulimia demonstrate a number of dysfunctional thoughts and behaviors related to body image and food management. Adolescents who are preoccupied with their own changing bodies and cultural emphasis on thinness often gain a new awareness of themselves through a support group approach. For those with seriously dysfunctional eating patterns, a positive group experience with empathetic and supportive group interactions may be the first step in a lifelong commitment to wellness.

REFERENCES

American Psychiatric Association (1987). *Diagnostic and statistical manual of mental disorders* (3rd Ed. Revised). Washington, D.C.

Anderson, A. E., (1985). *Practical comprehensive treatment of anorexia nervosa and bulimia.* Baltimore: John Hopkins.

Baldassare, M., (1986). *Trouble in paradise: The suburban transformation in America.* NY: Columbia University Press.

Faust, J. (1987). Correlates of the drive for thinness in young female adolescents. *Journal of Clinical Child Psychology 16(4),* 313-319.

Enright, A. B., Butterfield, P. & Berkowitz, B. (1985). Self-help and support groups in the management of eating disorders. In D. M. Garner & P. E. Garfinkel (Eds.). *Handbook of psychotherapy for anorexia nervosa and bulimia.* (pp. 491-512), NY: The Guilford Press.

Fairburn, C. G. (1985). Cognitive-behavioral treatment for bulimia. In D. M. Garner & P. E. Garfinkel (Eds). *Handbook of psychotherapy for anorexia nervosa and bulimia,* (pp. 160-192). NY: The Guilford Press.

Fishman, R. (1987) *Bourgeois utopias,* NY: Basic Books, Inc.

Garner, D. M. Garfinkel, P. E. & Olmsted, M. P. (1983). An overview of the socio-cultural factors in the development of anorexia nervosa. In P. L. Darby, P. E. Garfinkel, D. M. Garner, & D. V. Coscina (Eds.). *Anorexia nervosa: Recent developments* (65-82). NY: Alen R. Liss.

Garner, D. M., Rockert, W., Olmstead, M. P., Johnson, C. & Coscina, D. V. (1985). Psychoeducational principles in the treatment of bulimia and anorexia nervosa. In D. M. Garner & P. E. Garfinkel (Eds.) *Handbook of psychotherapy for anorexia nervosa and bulimia*, (513-562) NY: The Guilford Press.

Halmi, K. A., Falk, J. R., & Schwartz, E. (1981). Binge-eating and vomiting: A survey of a college population. *Psychological Medicine, 11*, 697-706.

Howat, P. M. & Saxtion, A. M. (1988). The incidence of bulimic behavior in a secondary and university school population. *Journal of Youth and Adolescence, 17*(3), 221-231.

Johnson, C. & Connors, M. E. (1987). *The etiology and treatment of bulimia nervosa: A biopsychosocial perspective*. NY: Basic Books, Inc.

Johnson, C., Lewis, C., Love, S., Lewis, L., and Stuckey, M. (1984). Incidence and correlates of bulimia behavior in a female high school population. *Journal of Youth and Adolescence, 13*, 15-26.

Larkin, R. W. (1979). *Suburban youth in cultural crisis*. New York: Oxford University Press.

Malekoff, A., Levine, M. & Quaglia, S. (1987). "An attempt to create a new 'old neighborhood': From suburban isolation to mutual caring." *Social Work with Groups, 10*(3), 55-68.

Mallick, M. J., Whipple, T. W., & Huerta, E. (1987). Behavioral and psychological traits of weight-conscious teenagers: A comparison of eating-disordered patients and high- and low-risk groups. *Adolescence, 22*(85), 157-168.

Mintz, N. E. (1985). A descriptive approach to bulimia. *Health and Social Work, 10*(2), 113-119.

Newman, B. M. & Newman, P. R. (1979). *Development through life: A psychosocial approach. (4th ed.)*, Homewood, IL: The Dorsey Press.

Pyle, A. L., Mitchell, J. E., Eckert, E. D., Halvorson, P. A., Neuman, P. A., and Goff, G. M. (1983). The incidence of bulimia in freshmen college students. *International Journal of Eating Disorders, 1*, 75-85.

Roth, D. M. & Ross, D. R. (1988). Long-term cognitive-interpersonal group therapy for eating disorders. *International Journal of Group Psychotherapy, 38*(4), 491-510.

Schwartz, R. C., Barrett, M. J., & Saba, G. (1985). Family therapy for bulimia. In D. M. Garner & P. E. Garfinkel, *Handbook of psychotherapy for anorexia nervosa and bulimia*. (280-310) NY: The Guilford Press.

Wermuth, B. M., Davis, K. L., Hollister, L. E., and Stunkard, A. J. (1977). Phenytoin treatment of the binge-eating syndrome. *American Journal of Psychiatry, 134*, 1249-1253.

Wooley, S. C. & Wooley, O. W. (1985). Intensive outpatient and residential treatment for bulimia. In D. M. Garner & P. E. Garfinkel, *Handbook of psychotherapy for anorexia nervosa and bulimia*, NY: The Guilford Press.

Structured Fantasy Approaches to Children's Group Therapy

Richard T. Walsh
Mary Ann Richardson
Raymond M. Cardey

SUMMARY. Structured fantasy group therapy makes use of the naturally occurring functions of the peer group to effect change through creative drama. The structured fantasy approach incorporates the use of symbolic play and group dynamics which are central to traditional group treatment. Yet, in recognition of the need for structure many children have, this approach includes elements of social problem-solving and videotaped feedback. The participants must learn and practice basic social skills, because they are essential to successful group enactments of collective fantasies. In this article we acknowledge the roots of structured fantasy groups, describe their various types, and discuss common group treatment issues. The article concludes with a discussion of the problems in evaluating group effectiveness, as exemplified by case study data.

PREFACE

The structured fantasy group work described herein, while effective with both inner city and rural children, originated in the sprawling twin-cities of Kitchener-Waterloo, Ontario, roughly 70 miles

Richard T. Walsh, PhD, is affiliated with the Department of Psychology, Wilfrid Laurier University, Waterloo, Ontario, N2L 3C5. Mary Ann Richardson, MSW, is affiliated with Peel Children's Centre. Raymond M. Cardey, PhD, is affiliated with Kitchener-Waterloo Hospital.

The authors wish to thank S. Franke, R. Freigang and A. Prabhu for their contributions to this work.

An earlier version was presented at the 1986 meetings of the Children's Group Therapy Association and the Society for the Exploration of Psychotherapy Integration.

southwest of Toronto. The Waterloo region has a rapidly expanding population of 325,000 which is expected to soar by the turn of the century. Although the region's cities have inner cores, like the other major centres in southern Ontario of London and Brampton-Missisauga, they are mainly characterized by vast tracts of middle-class and upper-middle class housing subdivisions. Poorer families, while constituting at least one-fifth of the population, tend to be less visible. In recent decades the overwhelmingly Anglo-Celtic-German background of the population has been fading, as immigrants from southern Europe, the Indian subcontinent, Southeast Asia and the Caribbean lend distinct multicultural hues to the human landscape.

Typically the families consist of two parents working outside the home, many of whom commute to jobs in other regions or in the urban centres of Hamilton and Toronto. Children and adolescents tend to be quite isolated from extended-family networks and might not have much contact even with their parents. Huge shopping malls, strip malls and convenience stores serve as focal points for children and youth, once school activities end. Neighborhood recreational centers and local social, health and mental health services are rarities. Rather, large edifices offering centralized services are the norm. But the social and mental health needs of suburban families are exhausting existing professional resources which generally are constructed along the traditional lines of a "private-practice" model of service delivery. Consequently, school systems are besieged by parental expectations to meet the total needs of children and adolescents.

INTRODUCTION

Several years ago we began to experiment with alternatives to traditional group therapy for children. Like many colleagues in children's mental health centres, we saw a changing population whose combined cognitive, social, and emotional impairments either excluded them from group play therapy or resulted in an inadequate therapeutic response. When group therapists in public agencies have relied on traditional group therapy modalities, they have frequently experienced major disappointments if not group chaos, since current referred children, particularly impulsive boys, seem to require predictable structure. In response to this problem we have drawn upon three distinct clinical models — traditional group play therapy, behaviourally oriented social skills training, and drama therapy — and upon the field of social group work. We assume that diverse clinical models can be integrated within a structured format to provide improved opportunities for interpersonal and intrapersonal development. In our view, development of an individual's social skills can be interwoven with the promotion of group cohesiveness through various dramatic media. After discussing other group treatment models, we describe the different types of structured fantasy groups we employ and then note the major problems we face in evaluating groups.

THEORETICAL AND CLINICAL ROOTS

Traditional Group Therapy

Psychodynamic approaches to group therapy for children essentially consist of play therapy in a group. In the original activity group therapy (AGT) model an atmosphere of unstructured acceptance provides children with an opportunity through symbolic play to regress, enact, and resolve unconscious conflicts (Schamess, 1976). Balancing group composition ensures that corrective identifications emerge, leading members to regulate themselves to achieve group acceptance. Passive limit setting maintains therapist acceptance and empathic support, assures safety and standards of appropriate social behaviour, and reinforces the development of impulse-control (Ginott, 1961). However, the corrective experiences provided in group play therapy are considered sufficient only for neurotic not for more disturbed or easily disorganized children. The lack of structure heightens the anxiety the latter experience to distressing levels which is incompatible with the essential therapeutic climate.

Activity-interview group therapy (A-IGT) was developed in an effort to meet the needs of children unsuitable for AGT (Slavson & Schiffer, 1975). A-IGT combines traditional play therapy with group interviews. The therapist directly explores feelings and offers interpretations to facilitate the development of insight and increased impulse-control. Although both AGT and A-IGT use members' interactions to achieve the therapeutic goals set for individual children, the primary focus is on the resolution of intrapsychic conflict. Improvements which may occur in a child's peer relations are a welcome by-product of the group experience.

Social Skills Groups

When group therapists in public agencies have relied on the AGT and A-IGT models, they have frequently experienced major disappointments if not group chaos, since current clinical populations seem to require predictable structure. By contrast, proponents of social skills groups directly train all types of children in the skills thought to be important to the development of satisfactory peer relations, on the assumption that children do not exhibit appropriate social behaviour because they lack the necessary skills. These social competencies are considered important, because the quality of childhood peer relationships is linked to later adjustment problems and referred children are not well accepted by their non-referred peers.

Clinicians and researchers in schools have developed a variety of behavioural and cognitive interventions based on behaviour modification (S.D. Rose, 1972), interpersonal problem-solving principles (S.R. Rose, 1987; Weissberg et al., 1981), and multimethod approaches (LaGreca & Santogrossi, 1980; S.D. Rose & Edleson, 1987). Social skills practitioners believe the group format to be more efficacious than individual treatment. Moreover, they note how their interventions can be integrated with the regular curriculum to serve entire classrooms (Nelson & Carson, 1988).

On the surface, social skills groups differ quite markedly from play therapy groups. First, the highly structured format provides members with well-defined goals and explicitly stated rules. Secondly, the therapist directly encourages peer feedback in the form of support, confrontation, and limit-setting. Finally, social skills groups tend to be of shorter duration than psychodynamic approaches. Interestingly, social skills proponents have directed little formal attention toward such traditional group dynamics as balanced group composition, multifaceted transference processes involving leaders and members, and the impact of termination on the group; in addition, they have tended to neglect the value of creative and metaphorical play.

Creative Drama

The third source for our work is creative drama (e.g., Dequine & Pearson-Davis, 1983; Schattner & Courtney, 1981). In this modality, the assumption is that the guided enactment of dramatic characters and fantasies allows children an opportunity for symbolic expression of thoughts and feelings as well as appropriate distance from their conflicts (cf. Wilson & Ryland, 1949). The therapeutic aspect of fantasy material resides in the potential for resolution of intrapersonal conflict, stimulation of moral development, and the enrichment of one's relationship to others (Bettelheim, 1977). Although the particular metaphorical vehicle may differ (e.g., clown shows, video dramas, fairy-tale enactments, puppet play), the intrinsic appeal of pretend evokes spontaneous responses across the age-span. Barsky and Mozenter (1976) observed how creative dramatic games seemed to promote greater cohesiveness and self-disclosure among children. In addition, other children's group therapists, operating from different theoretical perspectives and in different settings, have found that, when group members create dramas for videotaping and playback, both cohesiveness and self-awareness in the members are enhanced (e.g., Hoorwitz, 1984; Smith, Walsh, & Richardson, 1985; Stirtzinger & Robson, 1985).

Social Group Work

In our view each of the foregoing models contributes unique strengths which practitioners can blend into a potentially more effective approach than each can generate independently. Social skills groups offer the advantages of structured format, the effectiveness of short-term groups, the group's potential for enhancing the individual's sense of competency, and explicit skills training. Traditional play therapy groups permit children to enact and resolve their conflicts via the fantasies and feelings aroused through symbolic play in a safe atmosphere where group dynamics are carefully monitored. Creative drama provides ample opportunities for children to experiment with expanding their capacity for emotional expression under the protective guise of pretending. An integration of these three models, therefore, can permit the playing out of the children's conflicts and promote more competent social development, because the successful enactment of group-created dramas requires that the members practice basic social-emotional skills.

But this kind of structured integration of self, the environment, and fantasy exploration in small group interventions is not new. For over a half century social group work has incorporated nonverbal methods and activities, including drama (e.g., Boyd, 1939/1980; Middleman, 1968; Wilson & Ryland, 1949). Recent examples are: The use of creative games, a group photograph journal, creative drama, and discussion in a group for latency-age children involved in sexual abuse (Ross & Bilson, 1981); the use of photography, videotaped skits, and discussion of conflicts about sexual and racial identities in groups of early adolescent girls (Darrow & Lynch, 1983); disadvantaged youths' involvement in television productions of social dramas of their own creation (Shinar, 1983). Core principles common to social group work practice and to our structured fantasy approaches are the therapist's role as facilitator of group development, including the members' personal empowerment, and the group's emerging autonomy and power to effect interpersonal change.

STRUCTURED FANTASY APPROACHES

In light of the foregoing models and historical precedents, we attempt to blend and implement them in the following way. As the group members plan, rehearse, videotape, and then watch the playback of a drama they have created, the therapists guide them through the process by simultaneously: (a) introducing dramatic arts exercises and underscoring the importance of characterization, plot, use of the camera, dress-up clothing, and make-up; (b) attending to and directly addressing, if necessary, individual members' feelings and wishes about other members, the group, and the therapists; (c) commenting on unfolding group dynamics, such as cohesiveness or its lack; (d) employing social reinforcement, modelling, training in positive self-statements, and social problem-solving techniques to teach, when warranted, the skills required to cooperatively produce a successful drama. Consequently, adherents to different group treatment perspectives might regard structured fantasy groups differently. One might perceive a behavioural group due to the therapists' frequent use of structure and direct social skills training, another adherent might perceive a drama therapy group for special-needs children due to the emphasis on "producing a show," a third might perceive a traditional play therapy group due to the leaders' evocations of members' feelings and the attention paid to group process, while another might regard structured fantasy approaches as part of the social group work tradition of integrated activity groups.

Types and Clinical Issues

We have designed our group programme to meet the needs of the children referred to outpatient, family-centred clinics. Typically the girls and boys are impulsive, active, distractible, and easily aroused emotionally, although a significant minority present as shy, anxious, and withdrawn, and others have learning disabilities. The common denominator is that the children have experienced major difficulties in peer relations. Family workers make group referrals generally to promote social development, such as handling peer conflict, and to elevate the children's sense of competency and self-esteem. All the referred children and their parents have been involved to some degree with a family therapist prior to and during group membership. Group therapists assess the suitability of prospective members by discussing with them and their parents the purposes and format of the group and by clarifying mutual expectations. Therapists exclude children who are persistently hostile to the group's purpose, those who are so developmentally impaired relative to the other potential members that they could easily be overwhelmed cognitively and/or emotionally by the stimulation, and those who lack the minimum impulse-controls necessary for coping with small group interactions. At the group's conclusion, after consultation with the referring worker, the therapists review the child's progress with him or her and the parents.

Our initial attempt at integrating a structured group format with metaphorical material was the Clown Club (Smith et al., 1985). In this approach children are invited to become part of a clown troupe in which the group and the therapists assume clown identities, invent personal histories, and participate in a circus show. The Club employs a number of props (e.g., make-up and scrapbooks) to facilitate the adoption of clown identities. After some experience with this approach we replaced the circus motif in subsequent Clown Clubs with the idea of a travelling troupe of clowns, emphasizing group-constructed stories and plays which provide even greater opportunity for experimentation in roles among group members. The metaphor of the clown might work best for early latency-age children due to its inherent appeal for them. Many later-latency and early adolescent children (10 to 14 years) find the clown pretense "babyish." In response, we explored another type of structured fantasy. In the Drama Club members create videotaped dramatic skits which portray peer, school, and family issues. The dramatic themes can also encompass fantasy elements; for example, one group created a series featuring "video kids" lost in space who were rescued from the clutches of an evil monster by a friendly creature. The therapists function as facilitators for skit enactments and group discussions but do not participate in the skit themselves. Sometimes the members choose their own "directors" as cooperation builds.

Fairy-tale enactments seem to promote awareness of feelings and enhance creative expression particularly for younger children (i.e., five-six years old), but also for many older children and even adolescents. Popular choices have included Hansel and Gretel, The Three Little Pigs, and Jack in the Beanstalk, among others. Quiet, withdrawn children often portray "victim" roles, while more aggressive, domineering children tend to choose either villainous or heroic roles. Yet all members eventually broaden their range of experimentation with roles. In our experience pre-operational children would not be suited to the Drama Club or Clown Club approaches, because concrete guidelines for plot and character development are less evident. Rather, such children benefit from storybook enactments in which the therapists provide heavily structured supports. For example, group leaders narrate a simple fairy-tale with the aid of a picture book, then encourage the members to choose roles.

All of the above-mentioned approaches follow a similar format in session length and organization. The number of weekly sessions varies between 10 and 15, given our commitment to short-term groups and the evidence in the literature for their efficacy (S.R. Rose, 1985). Sessions are 60 to 90 minutes in length, depending on the maturity of the members. A session routine is established which consists of a beginning circle time for group discussion and planning, an activity time in which enactments occur, and, finally, another circle time for refreshments and discussion. This consistency and predictability are particularly helpful for the learning disabled and impulsive group members.

While the beginning phase of the various fantasy groups can seem much like a drama class as the therapists introduce warm-up exercises such as miming, mirroring, and fairy-tale enactments, the children are primarily involved in all aspects of group functioning from the first session. The therapists encourage the members to find ways of introducing themselves, to define group "rules," and to discuss how to solve problems arising in the group. The structured fantasy activities take the form of collectively created skits. Parallel processes are occurring in that, while the members ostensibly work on the enactments and the characters they are portraying, their dramas require considerable cooperation, problem-solving, frustration-tolerance, and attentiveness, all of which are problem areas for the members. Thus, the therapists encourage the group members to solve the problems occurring in the immediate group process in order to complete the group tasks: no skit proceeds until the group problem is solved. As part of this process the therapists often teach members how to listen to each other, usually indirectly by pointing out the process of who interrupted whom; but sometimes this instruction becomes quite concrete and direct.

By the middle phase of group development, as familiarity and cohesiveness build, members typically test their growing strength and autonomy. Pre-adolescents and adolescents, for instance, frequently attempt to engage the therapists in power struggles over group activities; sometimes they passively resist by attempting to abdicate decision-making to the therapists. At this turning point, with the therapists reflecting the responsibility back to the members, conflicts within the membership can escalate. Although the therapists guide the development of confrontation, negotiation, and resolution, their active role diminishes because members are assuming the functions of facilitating and supporting. Ideally, then, the group is relatively independent of adult control.

The final phase consists of the group creating more sophisticated and elaborate enactments. The increasingly complex dramatic material can become more realistic, as member trust and investment in each other reach a climax. On the other hand, the group's emotional climate can be quite stormy at this stage, because the group is also formally planning its termination. Due to the short-term nature of the group, the issue of termination is introduced in the initial sessions and developed in subsequent ones; group-constructed calendars and diaries can serve as concrete reminders of the group's eventual ending. Emotionally, however, pre-termination sessions are often laced with regressive behaviour, avoidance, and anger directed at the therapists. While the latter promote the members' verbal expression of their feelings, the members metaphorically deal with termination by enacting the "death" of their group through skits frequently involving natural or human-made disasters. When the final session arrives, the group usually carries out its planned ritual in a warm atmosphere. There is generally a "party" consisting of special snacks and, if the group desires, a replay of favourite portions of its videotaped skits. This occasion stimulates in each member recall of both individual and group progress since the first sessions.

A significant feature of our work with all age groups is the videotaping and playback of dramatic enactments. Video playback serves an "observing ego" function (Stirtzinger & Robson, 1985), that is, it enhances children's capacity for self-awareness. We have used playbacks as an opportunity for members to constructively criticize the quality of their productions and as concrete feedback about the members' group behaviour. Members' reactions to this material vary; for example, previously shy members who successfully role-play an extroverted character are often pleased by the video image they projected. Usually the therapists play back the production after one rehearsal so as to maintain spontaneity of performance, but some groups, particularly those of adolescents and of pre-operational members, benefit from additional rehearsal (cf. Dequine &

Pearson-Davis, 1983; Hoorwitz, 1984). The playbacks generally are not confrontational for the children, and even the youngest age groups are eager to see their performance. As Smith et al. (1985) reported, we have not found harmful effects of playbacks. In fact, with the members' consent we have shown edited versions of their productions to their parents during a "Videonight" held after a group's termination (cf. Shinar, 1983). These occasions seem to reinforce the members' pride in their shows and display quite graphically to their parents often previously unrecognized competencies in the children. Thus, according to referring family therapists, this intervention can serve to alter parents' perceptions and expectations of their children.

As previously noted, the structured format provides a safe, predictable environment particularly for learning-disabled and impulsive children who require a significant amount of organization. But overactive children require additional therapist precautions. We find it beneficial to reduce group size to four such members and retaining two therapists, to shorten session time to 60 minutes, and to provide picture books or videotapes to illustrate familiar children's stories, because of these children's limited attention span. Children with tenuous reality-contact (ego-impaired), who were deemed unsuitable for group play therapy, also seem to benefit. The metaphor combined with video playback and the particular organization of each session enable them to distinguish fantasy from reality as it occurs within the group setting. To illustrate, in one Clown Club, a youngster was referred due to her obsession with owls and frequent withdrawal into a rich fantasy life. During her group involvement she enacted her preoccupation by means of an owl characterization with the travelling troupe of clown performers. The removal of make-up, costumes, and props at the conclusion of each enactment helped her to symbolically discard her fantasy world and assume a place in reality-based group discussions and activities. Also, the members and therapists encouraged her creativity and spontaneity as positive contributions to the group. At termination the parents reported a significant improvement in this youngster's social interaction with peers and adults.

Another key dimension of structured fantasy groups is the role of the therapists. In our experience a co-therapy team is best, given the intensity of the sessions and the high activity level of the group members. Androgynous cooperation displayed between the therapists is an important aspect of their functioning in group, particularly if they are a female/male team. Co-therapist harmony frequently stimulates family fantasies in the members, and positive and negative transference is easily aroused, especially when the therapists play a confronting role. Accordingly, it is essential that the therapists allow sufficient time before and after sessions to review their thoughts, feelings, and fantasies about the group and their own working relationship. The success of the group, in large measure, depends upon the quality of this partnership. Although by no means essential, it is helpful if the therapists have had personal experience with creative drama. At the least, it is imperative for group success that the therapists be comfortable with the medium. Group members benefit from identifying with adult leaders who can be spontaneously expressive when clinically useful, as well as empathic and directive.

EVALUATION

There are significant problems inherent in designing evaluation studies in clinical settings (Cowen, 1987; Wickham & Cowan, 1986), such as the lack of untreated comparison groups. There are also conceptual and methodological problems intrinsic to evaluating drama therapy (Landy, 1984), such as defining what the drama intervention consists of. To cope with these difficulties we define our group treatment goals as anticipated improvements in: (a) the members' perceived ability to deal effectively with conflictual and non-conflictual peer situations, (b) teachers' and parents' perceptions of the members' social competencies. Accordingly, we assess group effectiveness by collecting data from several different converging sources and levels. Group members are asked to complete self-report measures of peer efficacy at the initial preparation interview and again at the group's conclusion. The members' parents and teachers are also asked to complete behaviour rating scales. Finally, psychology and social work interns, when available, rate the children's behaviour on interpersonal dimensions while observing group sessions through a two-way mirror; these data provide an invaluable gauge of the evolving group climate. The various findings obtained enable us to assess the progress of individual children and thus provide them, their parents, family therapists, and teachers, with feedback. In comparing pre-group and postgroup scores group means mask clinically relevant individual differences; thus, we analyze both group and individual data. The latter are particularly helpful in identifying those members for whom the group might not have been helpful or even harmful, as negative effects do occur in group treatment (cf. Dies & Teleska, 1985). Follow-up measures can further clarify the meaning of results for individual children.

Case Study

The following data from a Spring 1986 group illustrate the above problems and indicate some gains possibly related to the group intervention. But without a comparison group we can not conclude the group was effective beyond chance and maturational factors. Three girls and four boys, ranging in age from 12 to 14 years, attended a 13-session Drama Club. All the members were referred for peer problems, including aggression, scapegoating, and isolation. The therapists were a male psychologist with six years' experience in this modality and a female nurse with less than one year's experience; this co-therapy team had worked successfully in two previous clubs.

In the initial phase of the group's history, the members were mainly quite anxious and shy, although one of the boys quickly took on a decisive leadership role. Subsequently, the girls and two of the other boys began to make their own leadership contributions which resulted in numerous conflict situations. Intensifying the conflicts was the behaviour of one boy who began to express hostility toward the members and to the group's purpose. Despite this development, the group successfully produced a series of increasingly complex video dramas. In the final phase, with the exception of the latter boy, all of the members were highly attached to the group and were quite distressed about termination. By the group's conclusion, the quality of interpersonal skills among all members had substantially improved, including the oppositional boy who won peer acceptance when he became somewhat more cooperative.

Our overall impression was that this group was reasonably successful partly due to the high level of parental cooperation and personal responsibility displayed by the members regarding attendance. All told, there were only six absences across the history of the group, in more than half of the sessions all members were present, and three of the members had perfect attendance. As to formal evaluation, we administered pre and post measures to the members, their parents, and teachers. The members completed the Peer Interaction Scale (PIS), a 22-item measure of conflictual and cooperative peer situations (Wheeler & Ladd, 1982). The parents completed an adapted version of the Child Behaviour Rating Scale (CBRS), originally devised for teachers and containing 11 items pertaining to problems and 15 to competencies (Weissberg et al., 1981). The teachers completed the original CBRS for all but two members.

Looking at individual progress for the five of seven members with complete data, one girl improved on all factors; two boys and a girl improved to some degree at home, school, and in self-perception; and a third boy improved in self-perception and teacher-rated competencies. Six of the seven members improved on the PIS, while parents rated five members as less problematic and four more competent; teachers rated four of five members less problematic and three more competent. In the therapists' opinion, the boy with the most difficulty in the group would have benefitted from further involvement, only if he were actively committed to cooperative participation. The remaining members would have benefitted from another group to consolidate the gains they made.

As a group, the members significantly improved on the PIS with regard to their confidence in handling non-conflict situations, $t(6) = -3.12$, $p < .01$; and conflict situations, $t(6) = -2.53$, $p < .025$. But the parents did not rate their children on the modified CBRS as significantly less problematic nor as significantly more competent. On the other hand, the teachers rated the members as significantly decreased in overall problems, $t(4) = 2.35$, $p < .025$, while their ratings of improved competencies approached statistical significance ($p < .1$).

Clinical Implications

While these results are encouraging, we wrestle with such questions as, how much improvement can one realistically expect in functioning at home, school, and the community from participation in one short-term clinic group? How durable are any such improvements? Do changes on some measures but not others reflect improvement only in certain areas or are such results due principally to differential sensitivity of the various measures employed? Finally, which changes are most critical? As a consequence of this reflection, we are becoming more specific about treatment goals and turning to more specific measures of the children's social-emotional functioning. We have also observed that short-term groups in public agencies do have some decided advantages. Many children, as opposed to a select few, can be served. Relatedly, group members are usually at different stages therapeutically; for example, some referred children are ending treatment, while others beginning treatment are referred for group to provide the clinical team with a more comprehensive assessment. Furthermore, there is an opportunity for re-referral, depending on group members' progress, to consolidate gains, and to encourage the development of a leadership role for children who were prone to be scapegoated in their initial experience.

CONCLUSION

Structured fantasy approaches impress us as quite adaptable. A metaphorical vehicle can be selectively used as part of other group therapies occurring in residential as well as out-patient settings. Colleagues in child welfare agencies also have found creative drama to be therapeutic, particularly when they increase the ratio of member-to-leader support. The format can likewise be incorporated into longer-term therapy groups or collapsed into a daily schedule. As an example, we have successfully experimented with shortened versions during summer months whereby children attend 12 sessions over a three-week period; due to the intensity of the compressed treatment the members seem to rapidly acquire and apply more adaptive peer skills. In addition, recent interventions with school-based Drama Clubs seem to facilitate social problem-solving by enhancing generalization of social skills and self-esteem and lead to ecological effects in the schools (Walsh & Swanson, 1988). Based on this experience, we believe that there is considerable potential for similar school applications, systematically evaluated (cf. S.R. Rose, 1987).

Efforts to improve our work continue as we explore the viability of this integrative approach with the assistance of colleagues' feedback and formal evaluation. Certainly our explorations have led us to appreciate the curative power of fantasy in working with children. In fact, it is from their creativity that we have learned to reawaken this phenomenon within ourselves.

REFERENCES

Barsky, M., & Mozenter, G. (1976). The use of creative drama in a children's group. *International Journal of Group Psychotherapy, 26,* 105-114.
Bettelheim, B. (1977). *The uses of enchantment.* New York: Vintage Books.
Boyd, N. L. (1980). Play as a means of social adjustment. In A. S. Alissi (Ed.), *Perspectives on social group work,* (pp. 93-100). New York: Free Press. (Original work published 1939).
Cowen, E. L. (1978). Some problems in community program evaluation research. *Journal of Consulting and Clinical Psychology, 46,* 792-805.
Darrow, N. R., & Lynch, M. T. (1983). The use of photography activities with adolescent groups. *Social Work with Groups, 6,* 77-83.
Dequine, E. R., & Pearson-Davis, S. (1983). Videotaped improvisational drama with emotionally disturbed adolescents: A pilot study. *The Arts in Psychotherapy, 10,* 15-21.
Dies, R. R., & Teleska, P. A. (1985). Negative outcome in group psychotherapy. In D. T. Mays & C. M. Franks (Eds.), *Above all do not harm: Negative outcome in psychotherapy and what to do about it.* New York: Springer.
Ginott, H. (1961). *Group psychotherapy with children.* New York: McGraw-Hill.
Hoorwitz, A. N. (1984). Videotherapy in the context of group therapy for late-latency children of divorce. *Psychotherapy, 21,* 48-53.
LaGreca, A. M., & Santogrossi, D. A. (1980). Social skills training with elementary school students: A behavioural group approach. *Journal of Consulting and Clinical Psychology, 48,* 220-227.
Landy, R. J. (1984). Conceptual and methodological issues of research in drama therapy. *Arts in Psychotherapy, 11,* 89-100.
Middleman, R. R. (1968). *The non-verbal method in working with groups.* New York: Association Press.
Nelson, G., & Carson, P. (1988). Evaluation of a social problem-solving skills

program for 3rd and 4th grade students. *American Journal of Community Psychology, 16,* 79-99.

Rose, S. D. (1972). *Treating children in groups.* San Francisco: Jossey-Bass.

Rose, S. D., & Edleson, J. L. (1987). *Working with children and adolescents in groups.* San Francisco: Jossey-Bass.

Rose, S. R. (1985). Time-limited treatment groups for children. *Social Work with Groups, 8,* 17-27.

Rose, S. R. (1987). The development of problem-solving skills in children's groups. *Social Work with Groups, 10,* 85-95.

Ross, S., & Bilson, A. (1981). The Sunshine Group: An example of social work intervention through the use of a group. *Social Work with Groups, 4,* 15-28.

Schamess, G. (1976). Group therapy modalities for latency age children. *International Journal of Group Psychotherapy, 26,* 455-473.

Schattner, G., & Courtney, R. (Eds.) (1981). *Drama in therapy* (Vols. 1-2). New York: Drama Book Specialists.

Shinar, D. (1983). Television production as content and process in social work with groups: An experiment with disadvantaged neighborhood youth in Israel. *Social Work with Groups, 6,* 23-25.

Slavson, S. R., & Schiffer, M. (1975). *Group psychotherapies for children: A Textbook.* New York: International Universities Press.

Smith, J. D., Walsh, R. T., & Richardson, M. A. (1985). The Clown Club: A structured fantasy approach to group therapy with the latency-age child. *International Journal of Group Psychotherapy, 35,* 49-64.

Stirtzinger, R., & Robson, B. (1985). Videodrama and the observing ego. *Small Group Behaviour, 16,* 539-548.

Walsh, R. T., & Swanson, L. (1988, May). *Creative drama promotes social development in children and youth with special needs.* Paper presented at the fifth biennial meeting of the University of Waterloo Conference on Child Development, Waterloo, Ontario.

Weissberg, R. P., Gesten, E. L., Carnike, C. L., Toro, P. A., Rapkin, B. D., Davidson, E., & Cowen, E. L. (1981). Social problem-solving skills training: A competence-building intervention with second to fourth grade children. *American Journal of Community Psychology, 9,* 411-423.

Wheeler, V. A., & Ladd, G. W. (1982). Assessment of children's self-efficacy for social interaction with peers. *Developmental Psychology, 18,* 795-805.

Wickham, E., & Cowan, B. (1986). *Group treatment: An integration of theory and practice.* Waterloo, Ontario: Wilfrid Laurier University.

Wilson, G., & Ryland, G. (1949). *Social group work practice.* Cambridge, MA: Houghton-Mifflin.

'What's Goin' on in There?!?!': Alliance Formation with Parents Whose Children Are in Group Treatment

Andrew Malekoff

SUMMARY. The purpose of this article is to examine alliance formation with parents whose children are in group treatment. Aspects of beginning, middle and ending phases of treatment and related interventions with parents will be explored. The informing interview, translation of group development and dynamics and issues of trust and confidentiality will be emphasized within the context of parent-professional collaboration.

INTRODUCTION

How can we best orient parents whose children are about to begin group treatment? How can we explain the static that seeps from the group meeting place inevitably reaching the parents, piquing their senses, stoking their anxiety and testing their patience? How can we promote and preserve trust within the group while maintaining an alliance with the members' parents?

The purpose of this article is to examine alliance formation with parents whose children are in group treatment. The emphasis will be on encounters between group worker and parent during beginning, middle and ending phases of treatment. The community mental health center provides the backdrop (with one notable exception) for the practice described herein.

It is critical that the group worker remain appropriately accessible

Andrew Malekoff, ACSW, is Director of the Suburban Family Life Center and Substance Abuse Treatment and Prevention Services, North Shore Child and Family Guidance Center, Roslyn Heights, NY 11577.

to parents throughout the course of treatment to help them to understand the nature of group development (without sacrificing group
trust).* Parents can become empowered by gaining new perspectives on childhood and adolescence as dynamic themes are dramatically enacted in the group. The worker is provided with opportunities to promote competence and to normalize parents' perceptions
as their children pass through the long forgotten transitions of
youth.

BEGINNING (NOW YOU SEE IT . . .)

Following an appropriate evaluation, screening and recommendation for group treatment the worker's ability to effectively orient
the parents becomes critical in building the foundation for a working alliance. Perhaps in no other modality is there such ongoing
scrutiny about the value of the method itself. In group treatment
school age and adolescent children are seen in their "element," a
context in which power and control are clearly negotiable. This may
be an unsettling reality for the parent seated in the waiting room
hearing the noise bellowing forth from the place where their child is
being "treated."

The following questions represent an integrated sample of those
asked by parents when informed of the recommendation for group
treatment. After each question is a suggested response which must
be tailored to the uniqueness of the child and situation.**

1. Why a Group?

> Try and picture this: A group of six kids who have never met
> before drift into the local playground. One of them is dribbling
> a basketball and begins shooting. One by one, with no words
> spoken, the others wander over and join in. A "swish" is
> rewarded with the return of the ball for free shot. In awhile

---

*It is not the intention of this article to advocate for a particular modality with
which to work with parents.

**These questions are covered in the presence of the prospective group mem-
ber. Parameters for ongoing contact with parents are also discussed. Group members provide input regarding the nature and frequency of parental involvement.

they pick sides and decide on rules ("game's to fifteen . . . ya' have to win by two . . . winner takes it out . . ."). As they proceed they gradually begin to assess the strengths and weaknesses of each player on each team. Some do this consciously while others more intuitively. Spontaneous strategies are created, initiated, repeated and modified. They reward one another through both words and actions ("nice shot" or a "high five"). If the experience is worthwhile they agree to play two out of three.

The group is much like the team. The members share something in common and they've come together for a purpose. As in the example of the team, their strengths and weaknesses will emerge naturally and they will learn from and lean on one another.

In the above explanation, to the parents of group members, common ground, mutual aid and the concept of promoting mental health through ego building are introduced. The knowledge base is demystified and the prospective group members, depathologized. The value of the peer group is presented as a pro-active force capable of taking the initiative to confront problems and provide support.

The "choose-up" game is but one frame of reference serving as a metaphor for *what happens* in the group. The parents' own childhood memories of clubs, teams, etc., if they're willing to reveal them, are an excellent source with which to illustrate.

Such examples can also be used to help parents to better empathize with their children at a particular stage of development.

2. What Actually Happens in the Group? Do They Actually Talk About Their Problems?

Several years ago I worked with a group in which there was a twelve year old with a terrific imagination. The trouble was that he sometimes mixed up what was real with what he imagined. This created great problems for him when he tried to socialize. He was often the butt of cruel jokes which enraged him and lead to many fights. When any adult challenged his far out stories he would curse them and then withdraw. He would almost always end up isolated, misunderstood, angry and lonely.

As is almost always the case with group members he enacted in the group what he was accustomed to doing outside of the group. He *demonstrated* his particular problem. This demonstration was far more powerful than any intellectual discussion *about* problems. As the demonstration continued on a weekly basis the group "bully" emerged as he found his mark. And soon the group learned about *his* problem.

The solution eventually emerged after I asked the group if they knew what a "fish story" was. One of them obliged the others by defining the term. From that time on whenever the "exaggerator" started to "do his thing" the others simply held their hands apart with palms facing one another as if to wonder, "howwww big?" And the "exaggerator" couldn't help but smile and he would then proceed without further prompting to tone his story down.

So as you can see a great deal can happen without any words at all. However once the members felt safe enough to reveal themselves naturally, valuable discussions followed. We talked about exaggerating and bullying and their relationship to making friends, fitting in and feeling left out. The reality of their imperfections and the accompanying acceptance and support by their peers distinguishes group treatment. They can push, criticize and support one another in a way that no adult alone can. In the group they bring their outside lives *in* and they create something new, which takes on a *life of its own*.

Providing a "real" group treatment illustration helps the parents to "see" the worker and "group" in action. The group is described as a context in which the tools of social mastery are addressed. Despite any fantasies to the contrary parents are informed that their children will do more than talk in the group. But the fantasy lives on until the *static* begins.

STATIC (. . . NOW YOU DON'T)

Nolo contendre: a legal plea acknowledging a conviction but not guilt.

Time for a reality check. Despite careful thought and preparation and a wonderful presentation of the value and benefit of the group, parents are rarely prepared for the real thing. After the "honeymoon," when the members are on their best behavior maintaining their distance from one another, the storm begins to roll forth. As the normative crisis (p. 14, 15)[7] emerges and the members test out *what behavior goes* and *what doesn't* the level of noise and state of confusion accelerate rapidly. If there is a waiting room parents will inevitably hear the static. If parents of the other members also happen to be seated in the waiting room they may make eye contact for the very first time . . . and they will begin to shake their heads . . . and they will begin to talk . . . and they will have found *common ground*: 'What's Going On In There?!?!' *Laughter, banging, thumping, slamming doors, screams* . . . all serving to reinforce their worst fears about their children and about this *cockamamie group. Embarrassment, shame, doubt.* And *anger.* Anger at that guy or gal who sold them a bill of goods about what a wonderful experience *group treatment* would be for their children.

The parents' anguish at this point may be expressed in one of at least three convoluted ways, assuming that it is not communicated directly ("I'd-like-to-meet-with-you-to-discuss-the group") which it frequently is not.

(1) The *I'm-fed-up-disappointed-what-did-I-get-myself-into look.* The silence and facial expression here are stronger than any words. The purpose here is to elicit an explanation, as if there is already explicit agreement that one is in fact necessary about something in particular.

(2) The *you-go-wait-in-the-car-pivot-step-and-corral maneuver.* Here "junior" is sent ahead following the group meeting. The worker is cornered, usually in the presence and in earshot of colleagues, receptionist and clients, and asked the magic question: 'What's Goin On In There?!?!'

(3) The *this-may-be-my-last-meeting courier canard.* Here the

youngster becomes the parent's messenger. The purpose is for you to approach the parent, to make the first direct move. This usually occurs during the meeting following a particularly noisy one.

In any event it must be anticipated that, as in any treatment involving the welfare of their children, parents are legitimately and genuinely concerned about how things are going. The traditional model of professional as "knowledgeable decision maker" and parent as "passive recipient" (p. 33-52)[4] is alienating and intimidating to parents and an anathema to true collaboration. The slapstick described above, in which parents awkwardly try to get the worker's attention, is more a rejection of the all too typical inaccessability and aloofness of professionals than of any interactive inadequacy on the parents' part.

Periodic meetings serving as "refreshers" for parents will help to reassure them that what is happening is normal and expectable. "The parent struggling for hope demands that the professional accept the legitimacy of (their) struggle. The need for acceptance and understanding on the part of the (group worker) is of paramount importance to the parent" (p. 92).[3] It is not unusual for workers to feel challenged by parents. However ". . . the fact that parents are anxious, aloof or on the brink of tears or angry may show their reaction to the situation rather than their prevalent mood or style of interaction" (p. 149).[2]

Parents need to hear from us that their expressions of concern are not *out of bounds*.

THE MIDDLE PHASE:
MAINTAINING PARENTAL ALLIANCE
AND GROUP MEMBER TRUST

Once the group has become consolidated and is "working," parents are less apt to dwell on "static" and more likely to be problem focused. For the worker, a major dynamic issue is maintaining the parental alliance without sacrificing group trust. Speck and Atneave, in their work with networks contend that "the contract with the client system and the social network must be based on trust, not confidentiality" (p. 320).[8] "The traditional notion of confidentiality will not suffice as a visible, legitimate role as mediators and facilitators among . . . systems" (p. 321).[8]

In the following illustration the issues of trust, confidentiality and family loyalty are tested.

Ted had been a member of a boys' group for three years. He joined at age thirteen when he was transferred to a special educational setting. He had encountered daily beatings on the school bus and thus had become excessively truant. Ted lived with his parents and older sister who was the family "star," an excellent student and talented athlete.

By the time Ted reached his seventeenth birthday he was back in the home school district. He was gradually becoming "mainstreamed" academically and he had become a varsity athlete. He continued to be anxious and unsure of himself despite his success, which he acknowledged made him feel proud. Adjusting to part time employment, fitting in socially and planning for the future beyond high school were all concerns of Ted's.

Ted appeared extremely anxious and fidgety during a particular group meeting. He did not deny feeling disturbed about something but refused to discuss it despite the others' cajoling. Finally he admitted that he had promised his mother that he would not discuss *it*. Ted's position was respected and the group discussed the predicament of keeping family matters private. Each of the boys could relate to this as could Ted who described the feelings associated with the bind he was in: "I'm all tied up inside."

The worker asked if the others had any advice for Ted and they wondered if he, the worker, could talk to Ted's mom. Ted was hesitant, fearing he had said too much already. They rehearsed what might be said, emphasizing that Ted had not revealed the secret. He then agreed to the plan. The worker arranged a meeting. (Ted asked not to be included.)

Ted's dilemma was reviewed with his mom. Visibly relieved to have the opportunity, she revealed the secret and shared her feelings of shame, embarrassment and fear. Upon her return home she freed Ted to open up to the group.

At the next meeting, Ted revealed that his older sister had attempted suicide.

In the next illustration the "family secret" took another route.

Claude's father called and said he had to see the worker. It seems that his wife had discovered something disturbing under Claude's bed. The worker agreed to the meeting with the proviso that Claude be informed that his father would be coming in to discuss something.

Mr. K. entered the office holding a blue spiral notebook under his arm. He held out the notebook and declared "This is what I'm here about." He then placed it on the chair beside him and went on to describe its contents. It seems that Claude, sixteen at the time, decided to keep a diary of his sexual fantasies which, according to his father were rather explicit. Mr. K. remarked, "I didn't know he could write so well." The "diary" was discovered under Claude's bed, a place that his mother has been known to clean.

Mr. K., appearing mildly forlorn said that he didn't really think it, the notebook, was *that bad*. "After all he is a teenager." He offered the diary to the worker who declined to read it, adding that he trusted Mr. K.'s judgement. He asked Mr. K. if he thought that Claude might be looking to have a "man to man" talk. Mr. K. thought that that might be so and he agreed to tell Claude about his discovery and his meeting with the worker.

Subsequent to the father-son talk the worker met alone with Claude to affirm his knowledge of what had occurred. The purpose was to avoid any hint of collusion with his parents and also to reassure him that the choice was his about whether or not to discuss the incident in the group. He didn't reveal the details however he actively pursued discussions related to privacy and sexuality.

As we treat children in groups (as well as in other modalities) we must consider whether it "is ethical to work exclusively with one member of a social system while consciously excluding from the process of change those who will also be affected" (p. 321).[8] Rigid adherance to arbitrary standards of confidentiality work against the flexibility necessary to build and maintain a therapeutic alliance based upon trust and family integrity.

ENDINGS

Just as ending is a time for recapitulation and evaluation in the group, parents cannot be ignored during this phase. They have also struggled through the earliest stages of the group's development, monitored their children's progress during the course of treatment and often provided valuable feedback regarding their functioning outside of the group.

The group members may react during the separation phase (pp. 240-49)[4] in a variety of ways including: denial (we're not really going to quit meeting, are we?"), regression (early group conflicts which were resolved suddenly re-emerge), flight (missed meetings, premature departure), hostility (attempts to sabotage plans) and increased dependence on the group worker, despite gains in autonomous and interdependent functioning. For those youngsters who have experienced great loss in their lives parting may be especially painful as old feelings are reawakened.

Just as many parents are unfamiliar with what to expect in the beginning they are often unprepared for the end. By anticipating their child's reaction during this phase the worker can help the parents to consider and rehearse appropriate responses (i.e., discouraging missed sessions; relating empathically to resistance). Their alliance is re-emphasized here as parents and group worker join to prepare for the ending.

Parting also represents a loss for the parent who has developed a relationship with the worker and a connection to the agency. As with the children the intensity of the feelings are influenced by earlier losses. By exploring these feelings and working with the parents to discover and support alternative outlets for their children a healthy transition can be made.

Often parents will ask "can we come back if we need to?" By ensuring his/her availability the worker offers support as new experiences are sought. There are those who never return, some who call to say "hello" and make contact (re-fuel), and a few who do "come back."

In the final illustration Ralph Kolodny [5] provides a moving account of a group which was formed around a nine year old youngster who was being treated for hemophilia.

> I had met weekly with the group for three years in the kitchen of this youngster's home, he being completely homebound. I had also devised program activities in which I tried to reconcile the needs of the members, including the referred child, for expressing aggression with the limitations on aggressive behavior dictated by the child's dangerous condition. The club had met under the watchful eye of his mother, who had remained in the living-room during meetings but would customarily come in to serve refreshments and chat with the boys at the meeting's end.

> I was called by the family during the youngster's final hospitalization and remained with them until close to the hour of his death. Shortly thereafter I was a bit surprised to have the mother call and ask me if I could possibly get in touch with the five other former group members. She had not seen them in several years, most of them having moved far from the neighborhood. She wanted so much to see them. Through one of the former members who still lived nearby I was able to make contact with the others, now well into their teens, and, a week after the funeral, we met on the corner outside the house. They had not seen me in some four years, and a couple of them, lanky sixteen years olders, laughed and said, "Ralph, you shrank." We went into the house and sat in the kitchen with the mother. Her tears were matched by the warmth of her greeting. Where she found the emotional resources I do not know, but when I left the house she was still sitting with the boys and reminiscing about some of the lively and humorous incidents that had occurred in the group, four years and more before.

All too often we experience parents as a thorn in our "professional" side. We overidentify with the youngsters, perceive parents' questions as "the third degree" and hide behind the inviolable cloak of confidentiality. To get beyond these barriers requires a systems perspective, peer support, flexibility, courage and humility.

NOTES

1. Alexander, R. and Tompkins-McGill, P. (1987) "Notes to the Experts from the Parent of a Handicapped Child." *Social Work*.

2. Chess, S. and Hassibi, M. (1978) *Principles and Practice of Child Psychiatry*, Plenum Press, New York.

3. Dembo, T. (1984) "Sensitivity of One Person to Another." *Rehabilitation Literature*, 45 (3-4), 90-95.

4. Garland, J.A. and Kolodny, R.L. (1981) *The Treatment of Children Through Social Group Work: A Developmental Approach*, Charles Rivers Books, Charleston, Mass.

5. Healy, A., Keesee, P., Smith, B. (1985) *Early Services for Children with Special Needs: Transactions for Family Support*, The University of Iowa.

6. Kolodny, Ralph "Retrospective on Reaching Out: Boston's Late Department of Neighborhood Clubs." Presented at the Ninth Annual Symposium on the Advancement of Social Work with Groups, October 1987, Boston, Mass.

7. Lipsky, D. Kerzner (1985) "A Parental Perspective on Stress and Coping," *American Journal of Orthopsychiatry*, 55 (4).

8. Malekoff, A. and Kolodny, R.L. "Memories and Memory Building: Reflections on Group Work with the Lonely Child." (See the succeeding article in this book.)

9. Malekoff, Andrew (1984) "Socializing Pre-Adolescents into the Group Culture." *Group Work with Children and Adolescents*. Ralph Kolodny and James Garland (eds.), Haworth Press, Inc., New York.

10. Moore-Kirkland, J. and Irey, K. (1981) "A Reappraisal of Confidentiality." *Social Work*, July, 319-322.

11. Schneider, S. (1985) "The Role of Parents in the Treatment of Emotionally Disturbed Adolescents." *Family Therapy*, 12 (1), 35-43.

Memories and Memory Building: Reflections on Group Work with the Lonely Child

Andrew Malekoff
Ralph L. Kolodny

SUMMARY. This article will examine: (1) the application of group treatment in integrating and universalizing the lonely experience, (2) the loneliness of the group worker, and (3) the loneliness of leave taking and moving on. A special emphasis will be placed on the group worker's use of personal feelings and memories evoked during encounters with groups.

SPECIAL PLACES: THE AUTHOR REMEMBERS

There is no distinction whatever between marking out a space for a sacred purpose and marking it out for the purpose of sheer play . . . All are in form and function play-grounds, ie-forbidden spots, isolated, hedged round, hallowed, within which special rules obtain. All are temporary worlds within the ordinary world, dedicated to the performance of an act apart. (pp. 10, 19, 20)[7]

Schoolyards, vacant lots, street corners, makeshift clubhouses and stoops were but a few of the places of my boyhood past. These were the platforms upon which the richest of memories, sweet and

Andrew Malekoff, ACSW, is Director of the Suburban Family Life Center and Substance Abuse and Prevention Services, North Shore Child and Family Guidance Center, Roslyn Heights, NY 11577. Ralph L. Kolodny, MA, MSSS, is Professor Emeritus, Boston University School of Social Work, and Consultant, Department of Social Work, Ben Gurion University, Beersheba, Israel.

sour, were built. In later years it has been the countless hours working with youngsters in groups which have been most evocative of those special places and times. The associated images and scenarios provide, at each stop, a visceral reminder of my earliest struggles to belong.

I can vividly recall the year long effort, at age twelve, of trying to scale the grammar school roof, a local rite of passage. There was the repeated disappointment of falling short and the intermittent cadence of humiliating taunts bellowed forth by the older boys. But the image with which I attach the greatest fondness is that of the dangling arms of the few above, reaching out for my own outstretched hand, a majestically simple gesture emphasizing the mutuality upon which our time together was to be rooted.

SPECIAL PEOPLE

When one is cut off from human companionship, one discovers a deep reverence for . . . the one who stands by in the hour of need . . .

— Clark Moustakas

What about those whose only childhood memories are painful reminders of their social isolation, awkwardness and of their futile attempts to fit in? There are no outstretched hands except for those which are poised to recoil mockingly at the first approach. The peer group frame of reference for such youngsters is derived from the most circumscribed of settings such as the classroom. The clear cut structure allows only for programmed participation, but little ready access to the natural play activity context.

The purpose of this article is to explore the role of the treatment group in providing a new frame of reference for the isolated and lonely child, one in which memories of special times and places are built. In this context, the group is viewed neither solely as a means to the end of social competence nor as an end in itself, for "a therapeutic house is not a home."[8] It is the worker's commitment to integrating means and ends throughout the life of the group which enables the members to detoxify their earlier experiences with peers and to create something new, a benign social environment,* to be cherished in their memories forever.

LONELINESS AND SOCIAL ISOLATION IN ADOLESCENCE

Sullivan has implied that, despite our early sensitivity to significant others, it is only when we reach preadolescence that the experience of loneliness reaches its full significance.[15] This is fundamentally the result of the emergence of new interpersonal needs for closeness coupled with the loosening ties with parents as attachment figures. Brennan provides a comprehensive review of factors contributing to adolescent loneliness.[1] His survey is organized around three major themes:

> (1) Developmental changes (separation from parents, cognitive development, maturation, autonomy, disruption of self-concept and the struggle for significance); (2) Social structural factors (inadequate and marginal social roles, excessive rejection, excessive expectations and unrealistic norms, social comparisons within adolescent culture, the struggle for independence, changing family structures, poor parent-child relations and limited opportunity to make use of their talents); and (3) Personal traits (low self esteem, powerlessness, apathy, aimlessness and poor social skills).

In his work on loneliness and group development Garland refers to loneliness as a "cognitive and affective sense of longing and discomfort about one's sense of being, and one's apartness from places, states of life or communion with others (as distinguished from depression, anomia, alienation and aloneness)" (p. 97).[5] He offers the following propositions which serve to normalize our understanding of loneliness:

---

*In his discussion on "the capacity to be alone"[19] D.W. Winnicott refers to the individual's development of the belief in a "benign environment . . . through a repetition of satisfactory instinctual gratifications . . ." provided through "good enough mothering." It is in a similar sense that the mature group, as described herein, provides a kind of social holding environment.

(1) loneliness is universal in human life; (2) its character and identification vary in different personalities; (3) it appears and reappears in various forms throughout the life cycle and can produce growth; (4) it occurs along with cohesive and affiliative tendencies in all human groups; and (5) group workers must exercise caution in hasty or excessive promotion of either side of this relational coin. (p. 101)[5]

In an earlier paper Kolodny, in describing his work with the late Department of Neighborhood Clubs in Boston, comments on the group worker's mission of reducing social isolation in emotionally disturbed and handicapped youngsters.

It was not clear then, and it is not always clear now, whether, in a particular instance, the social isolation such a child suffers is mainly a result of fearful or hostile avoidance of him by his age peers, or whether it comes about largely because of his own tendency to reject overtures by others toward him . . . Whatever the source of isolation . . . (it is) itself a psychologically noxious element of profound significance. Rolling it back even if only to reduce the secondary effects of the child's central emotional or medical problem, the social withdrawal and avoidance that accompanies being "sick" in any form, is a task worthy of intense effort. Beyond this, there has always been the hope, viewed by some as a distinct possibility, that once social withdrawal is reversed, important psychological changes will follow. The child may then escape from those circular behavioral patterns in which he is regularly the subject of self-fulfilling prophecy of social alienation or the object of social attack . . . (p. 4, 5)[9]

Although by no means mutually inclusive entities, it is the point at which loneliness and social isolation intersect that the greatest longing may be experienced. The illustrations to follow will examine the following:

1. *The application of group treatment in integrating and universalizing the lonely experience.* The experiences of Ian, a member of a group set in an outpatient psychiatric setting and Billy, a member of a special school group will provide examples.

2. *The loneliness of the group worker* as a condition of both the work context and in the perceived incongruity of the group members' painful emotional lives and the "pleasure" offered them in the group meetings.
3. *The loneliness and warmth of leave taking and moving on.*

Special emphasis will be placed upon the group worker's "use of self" by drawing upon feelings and memories evoked by the encounters to be described, adherence to the discussion/activity construct in working with groups of youngsters and commitment to the spirit and practice of playfulness. (The illustrations to follow represent work with two groups of boys and the associated childhood memories of the workers, the authors. In the "outpatient group" the worker referred to is the author, Malekoff and in the "special school group" his co-author, Kolodny.)

ON BEING SEEN IN PUBLIC
WITH ONE'S PARENTS AT THIRTEEN

In loneliness, some compelling, essential aspect of life is suddenly challenged, threatened, altered, denied. (p. 21)[13]

Ian at thirteen and a half was a loner, a warm and thoughtful boy with some mild neurological deficits affecting his learning and speech. An avid science fiction reader, Ian's imagination and curiosity seemed to know no bounds. Ian was a tall, awkward looking boy who appeared, physically to be older than his age. He was referred by school personnel after making physical contact with a female teacher who became anxious that the touching was a sexual overture (as opposed to a plea for a nurturant response).

After about a year in the group the usually gregarious and talkative Ian appeared one day to be in a low down mood. The obviousness of his hanging head and uncharacteristic silence led to a volley of queries from the others. After a half hearted attempt to deflect attention he finally revealed that something had happened in school that day that made him feel physically sick to his stomach. After a barrage of requests: ("tell us," "c'mon what happened?," and so on) with some gentle encouragement this articulate young man with the creative mind went on to describe, in a hushed tone, what had happened during third period social studies class.

According to Ian the blackboard contained a message that made everyone entering the classroom ecstatic: there would be a substitute teacher. Spontaneous cheering was followed by a few moments of anxious anticipation. While most of the students chattered and waited to see who they'd be terrorizing, Ian opened his paperback and departed for some unknown galaxy. In a short time the volume in the classroom lowered and although Ian was "lost in space," he beamed himself back, closed the book on his thumb, expecting a quick return, and lifted his head to see HIS MOTHER standing in the front of the room.

As he replayed the experience he was thankful that no one knew it was his mother and that she didn't let on by kissing him or telling him that he had forgotten to take out the trash. The "numbness" and "sick feeling" that came on with the disbelief of seeing her in that context carried through the school day and into the group. It was a feeling that the worker knew very well.

> The worker's own parents found it difficult to understand what it felt like to be seen in public with them at thirteen. "What's wrong," his mom would say "are you *ashamed* of us?" This question always served as a marvelous tool for cutting to the quick and revealing in the worker, a lovely combination of anger, guilt and shame to add to his already growing embarrassment. He wondered, "did others feel this way?" In order to answer that question he began to make scientific observations of parent-teen interactions in local clothing stores. He chose clothing stores for his field research since there seemed nothing more humiliating, in his experience, than being subject to a middle aged bald man with a piece of chalk, playing with the crotch of one's pants, under the watchful eye of dear old mom and with a group of friends doubled over in laughter on the sidewalk just beyond the store window. His careful observations revealed that most of the others were just as squirmy and impatient as had been the worker. Were *they* ashamed of their parents? These feelings were never really discussed, probably since more profound issues like "who do

you like better Curly or Shemp?'' were under serious consideration. The opportunity to really talk about this at the time, to sort out the feelings and to normalize the experience would have been helpful, or so the worker now believes.

Moments like this seem to reveal new truths, shattering old perceptions and ideas. As the group members listened to Ian and, at the worker's suggestion, tried to put themselves in his shoes they started to resonate with him as they pictured their own moms or dads standing at the head of the class or in other ''compromising positions.'' Having access to all of the boys' parents the worker was able to provide impersonations within a variety of embarrassing contexts as imagined by the boys. Through the use of role play there was much good humor and ''kibitzing,''* but at the heart was the confrontation with the mourning of childhood identity, the gradual departure from the family cocoon and the realization of the ''lonely odyssey of youth'' (p. 98).[5]

INTERMISSION: 'SERIOUSNESS IS THE ROOT OF ALL MENTAL ILLNESS,'** SERIOUSLY***

Man is the only young thing in the world. A deadly seriousness emanates from all other forms of life. The cry of pain and of fear man has in common with other living things, but he alone can smile and laugh

—Eric Hoffer[16]

---

*Two classic ''social skills'' frequently observed being practiced by young adolescents in their natural groups: ''kibitzing'' and ''schmoozing'': ''. . . kibitzing is a competitive (activity) like repartee. A needle here, a bonmot there, a quip, a put down, a non sequitur are the kibitzer's stock in trade. For every kibitzer there is a victimized kibitzee . . . to schmooze is to engage in a relaxed, amiable, meandering conversation. Good schmoozing is an egalitarian, collaborative effort . . .''[17] The affiliation, reciprocity and flexibility inherent in these ''skills'' is enough to encourage their practice. Beyond this, though, is the style of discourse which allows for ''serious'' matters to be explored in a naturally playful manner.

**Maurice Schilling, M.D., New York City, N.Y.

***The authors.

As we leave Ian and prepare to join Billy, a word or two on
playfulness. Youngsters, socially isolated or integrated, awkward
or adept don't enter treatment groups prepared to engage in the
mode of discourse anticipated by many an uninitiated or impatient
worker. They do not exhibit the decorum expected by the disciples
of the "talking cure." Whether engaged in discussion, acitivity or
both, the playful-conversational style modeled by the worker will
go a long way in acculturating and sustaining the members' involvement (p. 15-17).[11]

In his treatise on "little league baseball and preadolescent culture" Fine points to the infusion of joy in one's work, adopting a
playful attitude toward it and transcending the formal rules of an
activity without breaking them (p. 189).[3] Just as the elements of
little league baseball (and like activities) contain components of
work and play, group treatment (and one might argue all treatment)
can be both worklike and playful at the same time.

> To the extent baseball (or group treatment) is treated as task
> oriented and externally directed, it is a form of work; to the
> extent it is flexible, free, and involves choice, it is play. In
> fact, it is both; each metaphor contributes to our understand-
> ing . . . The distinction between work and play as separable
> concepts is false. (p. 58)[3]

Children's natural play activity in formal and informal contexts
serves as an excellent frame of reference for the group worker. This
is especially so, but not exclusively, if the frames of reference are
the worker's own childhood memories.

THAT WAS THEN; THIS IS NOW,
OR JUST ANOTHER EXCUSE?

For many of the children's groups with whom we work as social
workers, day trips on special occasions can have a particular poign-
ancy, particularly if a fair number of the members are economically
impoverished as well as emotionally troubled. For the members of
the school group, coming into downtown with the worker on Christ-

mas, from the industrial suburb in which they lived brought not only pleasure but some pain as well. That one or another member would act out the pain, and that this acting-out might very well end up distressing the worker himself, was something he also came to expect.

Midway during the second year of the group, the worker took them in the van to see the Christmas display on the Common in the center of downtown, to be followed by refreshments. The day was crisp and lovely, and downtown was the festive place that urban downtowns still were in the early 1960's. Members and worker climbed out of the van next to a fine old brownstone, and Billy immediately ran over to the corner of the brownstone with a piece of chalk in his hand and, with an angry smile on his face, drew a swastika. This was a time for the worker to muster his professional objectivity, and in his best therapeutically neutral voice he asked, "What's that mean, Billy?"

But was there just the slightest quaver in his voice? Hints of anti-Semitism have a way of disconcerting Jewish workers. For this worker, they always brought him back to the sandlots and playgrounds of a New England mill town where he grew up in the thirties. Like most southern New England mill towns of the time, with their seething ethnic mixtures, his town was overwhelmingly Roman Catholic. It was among these Catholic youngsters that he naturally found both his friends and his enemies. The social atmosphere of the time and place carried a heavy charge of anti-Semitism, spurred on by the example of Nazism overseas. For the worker the happy memories of the playing field on the heights would always be marred. Twelve years old and happily wrestling with his close friend Bucky O'C. near the first base line, in the fashion of twelve-year-olds — and then the voice, the voice of mean Mike McD., seventeen years old, all five foot ten of him. "What are you doing playing with that Jew-bastard, Bucky?" At twelve one is not allowed to be a coward. Thus the inevitable. Several futile, furious swings up at the tormentor, the arch anti-Semite, followed by a terrible beating.

But the four-foot-seven ten-year-old standing in front of the worker defiantly with the chalk in his hand was not Mike McD. He was Billy, who lived in an alley tenement near the bus station, whose mother rarely showed emotion of any kind, and whose well-meaning father considered himself, and was considered by others, a total failure as he had lost one menial job after another. What must have been Billy's thoughts and feelings on being taken into the sumptuous world of downtown at Christmas time? His siblings were undoubtedly envious and must have let him know that they were. They must have had questions as to why he, the one who had brought particular shame to the family by his antic behavior in school and by being practically unable to either read or write, was being singled out for, what to them simply appeared as, interesting activities, two hours of fun, weekly. Under these conditions, Billy could not have escaped feeling a sense of separation from his family and strong ambivalence whenever a particularly pleasurable time was being offered him through the group. The drawing of this swastika was likely an expression of the ambivalence brought on by the gift of a good time, rather than a hostile personal attack. Suppression of one's own remembrance of painful things past was in order. Hadn't Erik Erikson written something about wedding clinical dispassion to moral indignation?

In control of himself now, the worker pressed his question, "What's that mean?" Back came Billy's retort, "It means I'm a big shot." Hands on hips he waited for his chastisement by the worker . . . "You really don't have to get yourself punished for having a good time, Billy," the worker replied. "It's O.K. for you guys to be here. You're supposed to have a good time." The worker's assessment of the situation and his comments seemed to be on the mark as Billy and the others relaxed. Then minutes later, however, down at the North Pole Village, with its bright striped wooden candy canes, circled by a wooden boardwalk, provocative behavior recurred. While angry mothers pulled in their children to avoid being knocked over, Billy began to run around wildly on the boardwalk, jumping up and smashing the overhanging wooden candy canes. Clearly there was the expectation of punishment on the part of Billy and the on-looking group members. The worker again felt, however, that, in line with Billy's current family experience, this behavior expressed not so much a desire to provoke, as concern about height and growing in general. An emotionally bland and unresponsive mother and a father whose work history was all downhill were factors not likely to provide positive responses to a youngster's growing up. The worker's comment to Billy, therefore, was simply, "I think you can touch the candy canes without jumping." Billy stopped, stretched his arm upward, and indeed reached the candy cane with his fingertips. He smiled, very pleased with himself. But then, grimacing, he said, "But I can't do it without standing on tiptoes." Continuing to relate to Billy's underlying feelings about how significant adults in his life felt about his growing up, the worker said directly, "Right now you have to stand on tiptoes, but, you'll see, there'll come a time when you'll be able to just lift your hand up and touch something that high without any trouble." Billy smiled again and slowed himself down to a walk, raising himself on tiptoe periodically and completing the rest of the trip without incident. He had learned, perhaps, that he could find adult figures in his life who were not highly ambivalent about his growing up. This is an important lesson. To this day, however, the worker continues to wonder whether Billy had learned anything about another important lesson, the one about swastikas? Somehow the worker always has difficulty remembering whether in the Erikson quotation the clinical dispassion or the moral indignation came first.

THE LONELINESS OF THE GROUP WORKER

The loneliness of the worker was partially due to the extra mural character of the work. The special school group was assigned a school basement room, which had a door with a small window in it, through which curious teachers would peep as they went by. This of course contributed to the worker's feelings of isolation and difference as they would always directly or indirectly question what he was doing with those kids. On the one hand they had been told that something "therapeutic" was being done. On the other, they could see that "all" that was going on was play. On top of this the teachers had no real idea who he was and where he was from, despite explanations from school caseworkers, and about the only status he had was that which stemmed from being slightly mysterious. At one point he took to wearing his Phi Beta Kappa key on a pocket chain to indicate that he had some kind of credentials. To be sure this may have reflected also his own sense of concern about what he was doing, about his own competence, whether he had any real knowledge about the meaning of what he was seeing and how to be helpful. All this kind of morbid self examination, which he found to be a regular part of his working life and which appears to be virtually inevitable, tends to emphasize the worker's feelings of isolation and loneliness.

Another potent source of loneliness for the worker is in the realization of the contrast between the awful emotional pain in the lives of many youngsters with whom we see and the offer and availability of "pleasure" offered by the meetings.

Tommy, who had begun to act strange and bewildered after his step-father committed suicide, and whose grades had begun to slip precipitiously was referred to the school group referred to above. When he moved to a new school he was given permission to continue in the group and the worker provided him with transportation. During these rides each time he would share with the worker his deep fears of how the stories they were reading in school about New England history would be repeated. For example, he couldn't rid his mind of the way "winter had killed" half of the settlers in Plymouth the first winter, and wondered if winter could still kill. In time he told the worker the full story of his step-father's suicide and the circumstances surrounding it. After many great times with his step-father things changed when the marriage to his mother took place.

"There was more fun," he said, "but then my step-father assaulted my brother and me" (in fact there had been an attempted homosexual rape). His mother had taken the step-father to court. Tommy and his brother testified against him in court and it was after this that "my step-father took the gas." Upon hearing this the worker caught his breath, and after a little bit, as they continued to drive, he said he guessed it must worry Tommy a lot sometimes when adults are nice to him and helping him to enjoy himself, whether or not some awful crazy things were going to happen. Tommy turned the conversation to Red Sox baseball, but shook the worker's hand when he left the car. The worker hoped that Tommy got the connection between what had happened to him and the mixed up feelings he had about being close to people (like the worker) and pleasure and what it might lead to, but one could never be completely sure. In any event, even though this seemed to be the correct approach, in emphasizing these connections, the worker was not always comfortable in doing so. This discomfort also contributed to his feelings of loneliness as a worker.

LEAVE TAKING, MOVING ON AND LOOKING BACK

As the group moves into the separation phase the worker can expect to experience mixed feelings of relief and concern. There is the relief stemming from the knowledge that the intense fatigue of years facing youngsters who are so often emotionally in pain and socially in trouble is about to be over. The concern arises around the worker's uncertainty as to whether his impressions of positive gains are illusory, or that they're unstable gains at best. These of course are the conscious feelings. The worker's unconscious feelings can be found in the chapter on "separation anxiety" in any book on psychodynamically oriented treatment.

The special school group of boys who were all twelve and thirteen when they were about to end, had spent three years together. The final meeting was held at a local restaurant. As parting time drew near Jack said he wished he could just sit there after supper and talk. The prior three meetings were highlighted by the force of the boys' denial and regression matched against the worker's efforts to encourage the boys to evaluate and recapitulate their time together. There was the recurrent, haunting question, posed in a variety of ways, of whether the experience and people would be forgotten. Would the boys forget one another? Would the worker forget the boys? Would the whole experience be lost?

On the ride back from the annually attended and agency sponsored summer camp a year earlier Jack's shutting off of positive memories was so immediate and powerful as to be overwhelming. He was a bright kid, much abused at home by a probably psychotic father and an often nasty step-mother who had lost her left leg in a car accident. He was the school bully when he was referred to the group. Shutting off memories of camp may have been a way of protecting them from being "taken away" from him at home through disparagement of them by his parents. Or maybe it represented his "hunger," that the pleasant experiences he had just consumed would no longer exist for him. Whatever the case, he couldn't bring himself to remember, wouldn't do so. A year later, he, of all the group members, was the one who wanted to bask in the warm glow of conversation about what they'd done.

THE WORKER: 'WHAT HAVE I DONE—ANYTHING?'

> A substantial statistical underpinning may be required by researchers and educators seeking evidence of the efficacy of a particular approach. For the practitioner immersed in the work itself, however, it is his or her impressions of the potential of the approach, as revealed at moments of its optimum impact on one or more group members, that persuade him or her of its worth. (p. 4)[9]

At thirteen and a half Sam was one of the original members of the group that, amongst others, included Ian. It was Sam, a well built and handsome youngster, who named the group the "A-Team" (after a television show depicting a fictional mercenary unit of war veterans). His dad had died suddenly of a heart attack within the year prior to Sam's joining the group. Although he was severely limited cognitively he became the indigenous leader, often identifying with the group worker. One of the boys, during a discussion in which they considered which part of the anatomy that each member represented, declared that Sam was the *heart* of the group.

The public school system decided early on that they could not accommodate Sam in his local district therefore he had to be bussed to a variety of specialized settings. These placements created more chaos than support for Sam. His periodic acts of aggression towards both students and teachers were probably more adaptive than school officials were ready to own up to considering the context. Dealing with aggression more appropriately was a goal for several members of the "A-Team" (the derivation of the name is no mystery).

Sam was a member of the "A-Team" for about five years. He

decided to leave during the year he anticipated graduating from high school. Several months after his final meeting an envelope arrived at the Center addressed to the worker. Inside was a letter for the worker and four more for the remaining group members. Sam concluded each letter with a verse from a song. Together the verses tell the story of Sam's time with the group.

> I used to be a renegade. I used to run around. But I couldn't take the punishment and had to settle down.

> I can't remember when you weren't there. When I didn't care for anyone but you. I swear we've been through everything there is.

> I can see you when you're asleep, you sleep so far away. And my arms will try to keep you but the heart knows it has to wait.

> I can dream about you, if I can hold you tonight. I can dream about you, you know how to hold me just right.*

CONCLUSION

> What we call the beginning is often the end and to make an end is to make a beginning; the end is where we start from
>
> —T.S. Eliot

The consolidation of experiences through recapitulation and evaluation serves, in the end, to accent the memories charted during the life of the group. The memories then become the historical landmarks revisited in the sentimental journeys to come. The once empty reservoirs, brimming at the moment of departure and subsiding some with the passage of time, will never drain completely. Always available will be the nourishment of reminiscence to be savored in solitude or swapped with others during times of nostalgic recollection.

---

*According to Sam these songs were performed respectively by Huey Lewis, Kenny Rogers, Jack Wagner and Dan Hartman.

When you were little you dreamed you were big, you must have been something, a real tiny kid. You wish you were me, I wish I was you, don't you wake up, this dream will come true . . .

— David Byrne

REFERENCES

1. Brennan, Tim, "Loneliness at Adolescence." In L.A. Peplau and Perlman, D. *Loneliness: A Sourcebook of Current Theory, Research and Therapy*. John Wiley and Son, New York, 1982, pp.269-290.

2. Byrne, David, "Dream Operator" *True Stories* (recording produced and performed by Talking Heads), Sire Records Company, New York, 1986.

3. Fine, Gary A. *With the Boys: Little League Baseball and Preadolescent Culture*. The University of Chicago Press, Chicago, 1987.

4. Frey, Louise A. and Kolodny, R.L. "Group Treatment for the Alienated Child in the School," *International Journal of Group Psychotherapy*, Vol. 16, No. 3, July, 1966, pp.321-337.

5. Garland, J.A. "Loneliness in the Group: An Element of Treatment," *Social Work with Groups*, Vol. 4, No. 314, 1981, pp.95-110.

6. Garland, J.A. and Kolodny, R.L. *Treatment of Children Through Social Group Work: A Developmental Approach*. Charles River Books, Boston, 1981.

7. Huizinga, Johan. *Homo Ludens: A Study of the Play Element in Culture* Roy Publishers, London 1950.

8. Keen, Sam. *Voices and Visions* (A Conversation with Joseph Campbell), Harper and Row, Publishers, New York, 1970, pp.67-86.

9. Kolodny, Ralph "Retrospective on Reaching Out: Boston's Late Department of Neighborhood Clubs." Presented at the Ninth Annual Symposium of the Committee of the Advancement of Social Work with Groups, Boston, Mass., Oct. 28-Nov. 1, 1987.

10. Malekoff, Andrew. "The Preadolescent Prerogative: Creative Blends of Discussion and Activity in Group Treatment" *Social Work with Groups*, Vol. 10, No. 4, 1988.

11. Malekoff, Andrew. "Socializing Preadolescents into the Group Culture." *Groupwork with Children and Adolescents. Social Work with Groups*. Vol. 7, No. 4, 1984.

12. Mayadas, Nazneen and Glasser, Paul. "Termination: A Neglected Aspect of Social Group Work" *Social Work with Groups*, Vol. 4, No. 1/2, pp.193-204.

13. Moustakas, Clark. *Loneliness*, Prentice-Hall, Inc., U.S.A., 1951.

14. Moustakas, Clark. *Loneliness and Love*, Prentice-Hall, Inc., New Jersey, 1972.

15. Sullivan, Harry Stack. *The Interpersonal Theory of Psychiatry*, WW Norton & Co., 1953, pp.245-262.

16. Tomkins, Calvin. *Eric Hoffer: An American Odyssey*, Harper and Row Publishers, New York.

17. Weinfeld, Morton, "How to Tell Kibitzing from Schmoozing" (letter to the editor) *New York Times* August 5, 1987.

18. Varner, Kathleen, "Termination as an Issue for Adolescent Groups" *Patterns in the Mosaic*, Proceedings of the Fourth Annual Symposium for the Advancement of Social Work with Groups, 1982.

19. Winnicott, D.W. "The Capacity to Be Alone" *The Maturational Process and the Facilitating Environment*. International Universities Press, 1965, pp.29-37.

Difference, Acceptance and Belonging:
A Reverie

Andrew Malekoff

SUMMARY. The purpose of this article is to illustrate the capacity of a group of boys, known mostly for their deficiencies, to touch one another by summoning forth their unique strengths and creating a time and space never to be forgotten.

INTRODUCTION

Matt was different from the others. It wasn't as if each of them weren't unique, but he was different. He had a working understanding of the stock market. His investments were modest but successful. He held three paper routes. None of his customers complained about missing their daily paper, although Matt did have some trouble keeping up with the collections. He liked to earn money and hoped to be wealthy one day. He had big dreams. Matt also laughed a lot. He often laughed for no apparent reason.

Andrew Malekoff, ACSW, is Director of the Suburban Family Life Center and Substance Abuse Treatment and Prevention Services, North Shore Child and Family Guidance Center, Roslyn Heights, NY 11577.

The author wishes to thank Marcy Dale, Jamie Lane and Darren Ericson.

Some years after the boys' group had disbanded, Tommy recalled the old days. He was completing a period of individual treatment and in the final months he reminisced mostly about the old group. His memories and perceptions about getting to know Matt were especially poignant.

What follows is intended as a reverie on difference, acceptance and belonging. The purpose is to illustrate the capacity of a group of boys, known mostly for their deficiencies, to touch one another by summoning forth their unique strengths and creating a time and space never to be forgotten.

FIRST IMPRESSION

Matt became a group member at age fifteen after reportedly having had individual treatment and neuroleptic chemotherapy on and off since age six. Upon first meeting Matt in a joint session with his parents, he appeared as a moderately obese almost electively mute and extremely guarded adolescent who maintained a steady rocking motion, punctuated by giggling, as he sat. Periodically his "far out" look was transformed into a fit of laughter as he arrived at some unknown inner destination. Inquiring about the source of hilarity didn't get very far until it was suggested that he try to control himself or share what was so funny. The worker told him that if he were to join the group he would, in all likelihood, have to do one or the other. He finally opted for the latter and said, in detached staccato, "I'm thinking about kids having sex with animals." And his laughter grew. As Tommy remembered him:

> He would startle you. Some of the things he'd say were shocking, they'd jolt you. But it was funny too. But it might hurt him to laugh at him. For him **it's serious**, for us it's funny. I guess that's not so nice the way it sounds. It's like someone tells you their mother died and you start laughing.

After a few deafening moments of silence the worker, frozen by the incongruity of the scene and trying to maintain his composure, glanced over to Matt's parents who sat expressionless, reminding him of the rural couple depicted in Grant Wood's "American Gothic." Matt's mother then broke the ice by saying that he was like this much of the time at home (and reportedly in school), especially during the past year, spending time by himself in his room, laughing. As the worker regained his balance he was carried back some twenty years to his own first "encounter" on the junior high school bus with another strange youngster, Arnold.

FULL CIRCLE FOR THE WORKER

It was at twelve and a half years old that the worker began the transition from elementary to junior high school. Public transportation replaced the five block walk to the lower school. The small, familiar and self-contained classroom was replaced by a variety of teachers and scores of kids. Junior high school meant sharing the hallways with eighth and ninth graders, kids that were beginning to look more like grown-ups than kids. A few of them were friendly, most were indifferent and more than a few were menacing.

Fear is probably the best word to describe how he felt during the early days in junior high school. Fear and loneliness. He was quite certain at that time that no one felt the same way. There was the daily nagging fear of forgetting the locker combination and of then being left alone in the corridor long after the bell had sounded. There was the chronic fear of losing his grammar school buddies to the seemingly more attractive and exciting kids who came from the six other lower schools. And then there was the acute fear that would begin to build at the close of each school day as he anticipated the bus trip home.

Up until that point in his life the worker had never met anyone with Down's Syndrome. The warning at the bus stop was to watch out for "the crazy maniac" on the back of the bus. Arnold was probably in his late teens at the time. It later became known that he boarded the bus after spending the day in a vocational rehabilitation program. The older boys in the back of the bus would egg him on to make sexually provocative requests of the younger boys. The combination of his unusual appearance and his "crazy talk" made finding a seat in the front of the bus a priority. Arnold was a truly frightening figure, someone to be avoided.

With the passage of time and the benefit of some perspective it became increasingly clear that Arnold was really a sweet and harmless guy, who was transformed into a monster.

COMMON GROUND

Beyond his lack of peer affiliation, the decision to try Matt in the group was based upon the worker's confidence in the other members' profound understanding of life at the margin as well as their great capacity for accepting difference (a capacity which far outdistanced the worker's own at their age).

> *It was a good thing for everyone in the group. It gave us a chance to learn how to deal with someone different than what is usually around us. He was different from most people we meet.*

All but one of the boys had no steady peer relationship outside of those in highly structured, non intimate settings. Each of them were described as "socially isolated" and all, to a greater or lesser degree, had experienced being scapegoated. Four of the boys were placed either in school settings outside of their home district or outside of the so called "mainstream" classes within their districts. Two members had experienced a series of devastating early losses. Despite the tremendous obstacles facing these boys, including the poverty of meaningful peer relations, none of them could be considered "schizoid." All were interested in making friends and all clearly demonstrated the capacity to derive pleasure from peer interactions. What they did share in common was an uncanny sensitivity and ability to empathize with the "underdog."

> *It wasn't difficult having him in the group – said Tommy – everyone has problems. You had to contain him – no help him to stop laughing. We had to help him, but we had to help each other too. Some people's problems are more noticeable. We had to help him to fit in better in the world.*

The others reacted at first with astonishment and then with anxious giggling and a touch of curiosity at the strange creations produced by Matt's imagination. In time they were able to confront Matt's laughter and to demand that he make an effort to control himself.

> *Did we help him? Not entirely, but a little bit. He did control himself a little bit better. Sometimes it seemed we were hard on him. Maybe we were just being firm. Maybe that is what he needed.*

Each of the five other boys then in group made personal associations with what one of them referred to as Matt's "silliness" and they recalled their own immature beginnings in the group. By using their own personal frames of reference they were able to reframe behavior that many would have labelled as "insane." Again, years later, Tommy put it aptly:

> *Everybody pretends but he has a deeper pretending. Like, I'll make believe and I'll know I'm just joking around. He's playing also but he's not joking around. He's doing it at a greater intensity.*

The worker encouraged them to recall and then proceeded to dramatize some of the idiosyncratic behavior which they described to bring it to life and to cut through the staleness of time. As hilarious as this turned out to be it also served to bring to the boys' awareness how far some of them had come (and still had to go), providing all with a renewed sense of hope. Since none of the boys had completely departed from their own "silly" beginnings, Matt's unusual behavior only served as a metaphor for the collective struggle of the group to achieve greater social competence. Matt was accepted on the same continuum rather than another plane, as was most often the case.

*Maybe he was like a radio, tuning in and tuning out, his plane and our plane or he would be in both planes at once. And sometimes he'd **just** be with us.*

THE PEOPLE'S COURT

The group had been meeting for about a year when the oldest member, the indigenous leader, carried a folder into the meeting. He opened the folder, presented its contents (papers) and announced that he had a case to present for the "People's Court." Without hesitation he assigned the worker to be the judge, himself as the attorney for the defense and the others in a variety of roles (prosecuting attorney, court officer, defendant, plaintiff, witness). The others reluctantly agreed to cooperate. Their awkwardness was played out through giggling and horseplay but they continued. This activity was introduced following many discussions of favorite television programs of which the "People's Court" was just one. The members had also been examining their behavior outside of the group after it had been discovered that two of the boys had been suspended from school for fighting.

For the next several weeks the same boy brought in new cases to be heard. The initial resistance to continue this exercise was diminished as the sophistication of the activity developed. Creative possibilities emerged: (a) members assumed unfamiliar roles (i.e., eventually the judgeship was shared and assigned to the most ambivalent member, thus he had to become unequivocal and judicious; the least assertive group member took a turn as the prosecuting attorney, etc.); (b) in addition to dealing with the facts of artificial cases, members readily assumed "third person" roles in which they were "cross-examined" about their "real selves." Experiences and feelings which seemed otherwise inaccessible emerged more readily in the "third person" context. Conflicts which occurred both in and out of the group setting were placed on the docket.

As did most local newsboys, Matt used a shopping cart to deliver his papers. Although he denied that he was referring to himself, he began to obsessively question the legality of the practice. Despite the others' reassurance that this wasn't "breaking the law" he persisted for weeks. Once instituted, the mock trial provided a new context for the discussion. An impartial jury consisting of all of the group members was empaneled to reflect on and decide upon this case.

The result was a lively debate which concluded with a finding that the "defendant" was innocent of any crime. Distinctions were drawn between this and other related behavior. After the trial he never raised this issue again, but he did return to the "People's Court." As a young adult looking back, Tommy indicated that he had understood Matt's struggle with reality.

> *Life could be hard for him, kind of. But maybe not. It may be hard but he may not feel it. I guess it is hard, he might need someone to depend on, a crutch. Certain people may not be very understanding. They may tease him or hurt him, maybe even physically. They're stupid. Maybe he won't need anyone, but he probably will. Everybody does.*

After awhile the group lost interest in the activity, especially as a weekly enterprise, however it became a valuable tool to return to as the group progressed. The mock trial provided the boys with an opportunity to experiment with values, and to gain experience in critical thinking, problem solving and decision making. As one might expect the activity was filled with humor which only served to bring the boys, including Matt, closer together as they learned to enjoy and appreciate one another.

R.S.V.P.

In addition to discussion and role playing activities, the group periodically held parties at the Center. The members took responsibility for the planning. After a time and several parties and "trials" later Matt came to one meeting awkwardly clutching several brightly colored envelopes. As he handed out these invitations for a party to celebrate his sixteenth birthday, the others fell silent. And then each of them in their own words said they weren't sure if they could make it, for one reason or another. Matt seemed unfazed. He grunted inaudibly and shrugged his shoulders. The worker simply suggested that they R.S.V.P., as requested on the cards.

Matt's mother later revealed that the scene at her home on the day of the party was one she hadn't experienced for at least the past ten of Matt's sixteen years. All of the boys showed up.

The birthday party was a turning point in the collateral work with Matt's parents whose own loneliness emerged as they began to acknowledge their shattered dreams, which were covered over with year of denial. It also enabled the worker's greater access to Matt's younger brother who was so confused about his big brother. The family's relationship to the Center did not erase their loneliness however it reduced their isolation thus helping them to accept and move forward.

> *It was fun. It was nice. There was one thing bad. I ate so many potato chips I couldn't eat the pizza. He was quiet. He knew we were there and acknowledged us. Matt was quiet. He knew we were there. But he wasn't there, kind of. We were telling jokes or playing frisbee and he was just there. He asked us if we wanted anything.*

BOOK REVIEWS

Introduction

In 1984 Ralph L. Kolodny and James A. Garland, introduced *Groupwork with Children and Adolescents*[1] as follows:

> Groupwork practice with children and youth has exerted a strong influence on the value system, conceptual framework and technology of social work with groups. From its early emergence in settlement houses, community centers and child care institutions, through its street corner gang period and into its latter day proliferation in public schools, clinics and residential treatment programs, it has been both a creative pace-setter and a neglected step-child of the profession . . .

Some years earlier Saul Bernstein and his colleagues (two of whom were Garland and Kolodny) at the Boston University School of Social Work compiled two volumes which epitomize the influence noted above.

I was first introduced to these works as a VISTA volunteer who had no social work background. Although unfamiliar with the more technical language, I benefited mostly from the richness of the anecdotal material. I began to discover that I wasn't alone and that there was a method to the madness I had been experiencing in my work with youth. Over the years I have often returned to *Explorations* and *Further Explorations* for guidance and validation.

Andrew Malekoff
North Shore Child
and Family Guidance Center
Roslyn Heights, NY 11577

NOTE

1. Kolodny, Ralph L. and Garland, James A. *Group Work with Children and Adolescents*. The Haworth Press, New York 1984.

The Boston Group:
A Retrospective

EXPLORATIONS IN GROUP WORK. Saul Bernstein, ed. *Practitioner Press, 20 Overbrook Farm Rd., Bloomfield, CT 06002.*

FURTHER EXPLORATIONS IN GROUP WORK. Saul Bernstein, ed. *Practitioner Press, 20 Overbrook Farm Rd., Bloomfield, CT 06002.*

In 1959 under the guidance of Saul Bernstein, then professor and Chair of the Group Work Department, Boston University School of Social Work, the Group Work Theory Committee was convened, a unique and creative combination of practitioners, (now become teachers) and theoreticians. Their purpose was to advance knowledge building (theory development) in the service of improved social group work practice. They aimed for middle range theory, neither too descriptive nor too abstract, but useful to the worker with live community groups. This collection of about ten practitioners and teachers became a cohesive working group, developing through the stages so effectively conceptualized in the "Boston model" of group development; and reminiscent of the early efforts of practitioners and theoreticians of several disciplines in Chicago and elsewhere to develop practice theory.

The processes of this theory building effort appear to have been an analogue of good group work practice: exploring and defining the dimensions of the common goal, assessing the resources, building on the known and encouraging flexible and creative individual efforts in behalf of the group goal.

This open process resulted in four practice issues being identified:

115

1. exploration and the establishment of a working agreement;
2. a model for stages of development in social work groups;
3. conflict and group work;
4. decision making and group work.

Each of these subjects represented, and continue to be, crucial practice tasks to be addressed. The authors built from practice to principles, utilizing case vignettes to illustrate their points. The ensuing articles read very clearly and practically today, with sufficient abstraction to be transferred to current social group work practice. The authors' basic theoretical frame for understanding is ego psychological, not heavily psychoanalytic, but taking into account past experiences, family contexts, and social (especially agency) contexts and purposes. The participation of case work and community faculty in the group deliberations served to enhance their more holistic orientation.

For our purposes, in this paper of the publication, much of the original case material is drawn from practice with children's and adolescent's groups. The topics chosen for development in *Explorations* seem particularly relevant to adolescent struggles to accept help from an adult worker, struggles for autonomy, for conflict resolution and decision making. The emphasis on work with "natural" groups in their natural community habitat also would seem to ease the process of applicability and incorporation of practice principles to current work with groups.

While there were some personnel changes during the preparation of *Further Explorations*, the form of theory development continued. Although content becomes more specific there is a clear focus on the whole context of life: the individual, the family, the group and the larger social setting, and the interchange and influence between and among these entities. For the practitioner, the Theory Group's decision to stay with "real groups" in agencies rather than utilize laboratory groups makes easier the translation of theory into practice. The articles in the second volume demonstrate both a growing complexity of analyses and understanding, and an attempt to apply earlier generalized principles to specific populations: institutionalized persons with mental illness, handicapped children, disturbed children. In addition, worker and member tasks such as group composition, dealing with scapegoating, goal formulation, and basic practice values are explored in depth. These complement and expand the practice knowledge of the first volume. These issues, like the first ones, are continuing concerns for the group work practitioner. The articles, while suggesting points to be considered in making a practice plan, avoid prescription and encourage further inquiry and testing by the practitioner.

The papers in these two volumes attest to the power and creativity, as well as to the time and commitment, required to produce sound social group work practice theory. Amazingly, the developments of thirty years ago seem as sound and practical for working with today's youth, living in suburban and advantaged surroundings, as they have proved to be in working with inner city children and youth.

This fruitful collaboration of skilled practitioners and teachers of practice should be continued, supported and expanded as we attempt to enhance both theory and practice of social group work. The collaborative group experience may be as instructive to us in understanding and treasuring both process and product in social group work.

Elizabeth Lewis, PhD
Professor
Department of Social Work
Cleveland State University

For Product Safety Concerns and Information please contact our EU
representative GPSR@taylorandfrancis.com
Taylor & Francis Verlag GmbH, Kaufingerstraße 24, 80331 München, Germany

www.ingramcontent.com/pod-product-compliance
Lightning Source LLC
Chambersburg PA
CBHW050533270326
41926CB00015B/3210

9 781138 051348